Mr Cocker has, for over twenty-five years, made a speciality of annuals, and he is the Superintendent of the well-known Villa Taranto gardens in Northern Italy, where tens of thousands of annuals are grown each year for the benefit of visitors, and where there is a unique range of these popular and useful plants, collected from all over the world.

In this book Mr Cocker shows how wide the range of annuals really is, for he describes many hundreds, many of which are undeservedly neglected. It is to be hoped that through the enthusiasm of the author, many more gardeners will devote space to these beautiful, easily cultivated plants.

The preparation of the soil and the cultivation of annuals are fully described, and lists are given of annuals of all types and for various situations, while Chapter Six of the book is devoted to a descriptive alphabetical list.

An Amateur Gardening Handbook

THIS BOOK

IS NO 4 OF THE AMATEUR GARDENING HANDBOOKS

others in the series are

NEW TITLES ARE ADDED FROM TIME TO TIME

ANNUAL FLOWERS

HENRY COCKER, A.H.R.H.S.

Superintendent of the Villa Taranto gardens

4

W. H. & L. COLLINGRIDGE LTD

2-10 TAVISTOCK STREET COVENT GARDEN LONDON WC2

FIRST PUBLISHED IN 1953

The Amateur Gardening Handbooks
are published by
W. H. & L. Collingridge Limited
2-10 Tavistock Street London WC2
and printed and bound in England by
Hazell Watson & Viney Limited
Aylesbury and London

SECOND IMPRESSION 1957

CONTENTS

ILLUSTRATIONS

CHAPTER ONE

THE PLACE OF ANNUALS
IN THE GARDEN

THE plants mentioned in this book are, with certain exceptions, true annuals. That is, their seeds can be sown, they will germinate, reach maturity, bloom and produce seed again within a year or less, and then die. The period between seed sowing and seed collecting varies from a few weeks to several months, and this brief life makes annual plants particularly suitable for producing an abundance of brightly coloured flowers in the garden between spring and autumn. The exceptions are plants which, while not strictly annuals, can conveniently be grown as such although they really may be biennials or even perennials.

Zinnias are a typical example of true annuals, but it is dangerous to become dogmatic on the subject of what is an annual and what is not. Many gardeners firmly believe that such plants as Antirrhinums and Petunias are annuals, whereas under favourable conditions each of these plants will live for many years, particularly in old walls. It is, however, more convenient to grow them as annuals.

The value of annuals in the garden is so great, and their range of size, flowering period and colour is so vast, that it is difficult to conceive a small garden which does not rely upon annuals for the major part of its summer display. Big estates can devote large areas to flowering trees and shrubs and seasonal flowers, but where the maximum effect has to be achieved in the minimum space there is nothing to equal a well-balanced collection of annuals. Suitable varieties can be found for almost every type of garden and situation, and in Chapter Four selected annuals are suggested for special purposes. Generally, annuals prefer an open, sunny position in well-drained soil. They can be grown either in formal beds or allowed to naturalize in irregular groups or can be grown purely for the supply of cut blooms.

Annuals can be used as a groundwork for bulbs, such as pansies among tulips; there are climbing annuals suitable for making a screen or for covering trellis-work; they can be used in crazy-paving and in the rock garden; and will extend the flowering period of herbaceous borders. Others are useful for window-boxes and hanging baskets, while many can serve as edging plants or for providing splashes of colour among spring-flowering shrubs long after the latter have finished flowering. An entire border devoted to annuals can be a glorious sight, and as much pleasure and interest can be had from planning this as from planning an herbaceous border.

It is, however, as a bedding plant that the annual proves its greatest value, and our private gardens, public parks and open spaces would indeed be dull places without their beds of Salvias, Antirrhinums, Petunias, Ageratum, Tagetes, Verbenas and the like. Beautiful as these subjects are, there are many other equally attractive annuals which, for one reason or another, are practically unknown or rarely cultivated. Many of these will be found in Chapter Six.

CHAPTER TWO

THE CULTIVATION OF HARDY ANNUALS

FOR the purpose of garden cultivation, annuals are roughly divided into two broad groups: hardy annuals and half-hardy annuals. This division is purely artificial, and is governed by climatic conditions rather than by any botanical differences. There can be a considerable amount of overlapping between the two groups, and in warmer districts many so-called half-hardy annuals can be treated as hardy annuals, while in bleak areas some hardy annuals are better if treated as half-hardy.

Hardy annuals will withstand a slight amount of frost, and can be sown direct in the open ground; while half-hardy annuals require to be raised under glass, either in frames or a cool greenhouse; or else sown in the open ground much later in the season. Hardy annuals are probably the easiest of all plants to grow. Once the parent plants have been established, they will even sow themselves and produce excellent new plants each year if the surrounding soil is not disturbed too violently. Tobacco plants, Shirley Poppies, Kochias and Portulacas will often give magnificent results in this way. In my own garden I sowed some seeds of the lovely crimson *Nicotiana Sanderae* about ten years ago, near the edge of a path, and every year since a fine batch of self-sown seedlings has appeared and provided a wealth of bloom.

The Site The preparations necessary for sowing are

simple, except for Sweet Peas, which will be dealt with later. When selecting a site, an open, sunny position should be chosen, and this point cannot be over emphasized. Only poor results will be obtained if cultivation is attempted under overhanging trees or in perpetual shade of buildings. When new beds are planned, these should be well dug and manured during the previous autumn or winter, with the surface left rough and unbroken so that it can be well weathered during the winter months. Annuals are not generally gross feeders, and very rich soil can even be a disadvantage. They do, however, appreciate a good soil, and if the chosen site is unduly poor it can be enriched with old manure, rotted leaves or material from the compost heap. Light soils are more suitable than heavy soils, and the latter can be improved by the incorporation of peat, leaf-soil or fine ashes.

When and How to Sow   Seeds can be sown in the open ground, but the time depends on both weather and situation. Seeds can generally be sown towards the end of March or early in April, when the risk of hard frost is over. A calm day should be chosen when the soil is moderately moist and easily worked. The soil should be firm and raked as fine as possible before sowing, and the smallest seeds only covered by gently raking them into the surface of the soil. Larger seeds, such as Nasturtiums, can be covered by about 1 inch of soil.

When sowing seeds of annuals in a mixed border or in a border devoted entirely to annuals, it is effective to sow each variety in a patch of irregular shape, but the patches should have their boundaries marked by small sticks

10

before sowing is actually carried out. If annuals are being grown for cut blooms, they are best sown in rows. After sowing, lightly press down the soil surface and give a gentle watering. Where birds or cats are liable to be a nuisance, it is advisable to lay a few twigs on the freshly sown soil. No matter how much care is taken in sowing, however, all the good work will be wasted if seeds are sown too thickly. Sow as thinly as reasonably possible, bearing in mind that each seed can produce a plant capable of covering an area at least equal to that occupied by this book when laid flat open on a table.

Weeding and Thinning Each of these most important operations requires patience and care, and should be carried out as early as possible in order to avoid disturbance to the roots of the plants which are left. On most soils it is easier to carry out these operations when the ground is moist. When thinning out it is as well to remember that a few, well-grown, fully-developed plants make a better show than a mass of overcrowded plants which are all suffocating each other in their struggle for growing space. As they grow, most annuals will benefit from the support of a few small sticks or twigs; such help will be of special value during heavy rain or strong wind. Still later, the regular removal of dead flower heads will lengthen the flowering period of most annuals.

Sweet Peas These will repay the extra work involved in their cultivation, as they are certainly among the finest of all our annuals, especially for cut blooms and show purposes. They require rich, well-prepared soil in an open, sunny position. Holes or trenches should be dug out to a depth of from $1\frac{1}{2}$ to 2 ft. during the previous autumn and a good layer of well-rotted manure placed in the bottom. The holes can then be refilled with a mixture of soil and manure, and left until spring, when the young Sweet Pea seedlings can be planted. The most convenient time for sowing Sweet Peas is late January or early February. Sow two or three seeds in each 3-inch pot, and keep in a cool greenhouse or a well-protected frame until germination takes place. They can then be gradually hardened off by exposing them more and more to normal, outside temperature until ready for planting in March or April, according to the weather. At planting time the seedlings should be from 4 to 6 inches high, and it is best to leave only two young plants in each pot. It is advisable to support them with a few small twigs for a while before planting. From 12 to 15 inches should be allowed between each pot of plants, whether they are grown in rows or in groups, say round the perimeter of a circle. Plants can either be supported by the orthodox peasticks or trained up strings, wire or netting. For early flowering, sow seeds in the same manner in autumn and winter in a cold frame.

When grown for exhibition the plants should be restricted to a single stem and all side shoots removed. For ordinary garden purposes the plants can be left to grow naturally, but ample support must be given and all dead flowers regularly removed. If an excessive amount of foliage and surplus tendrils are produced, it will be beneficial to cut out some of this.

CHAPTER THREE

THE CULTIVATION
OF HALF-HARDY ANNUALS

WHILE the cultivation of half-hardy annuals calls for slightly more attention than hardy annuals, there are no very great difficulties, and the extra facilities required can be confined to modest proportions. As their name suggests, half-hardy annuals will not tolerate frost, especially during the seedling stage, but they can be sown in the open in May, when the danger of frost is over, but this sometimes reduces their growing period so that they do not have sufficient time to reach maturity before the summer is over.

The only practical alternative is to sow half-hardy annuals in spring in a well-protected frame or, better still, in a cool greenhouse, and so continue to give the young seedlings protection until the weather is mild enough to plant them out. Even certain hardy annuals will give better results if raised under glass, as they can be sown earlier and the young plants are not subject to the vagaries of spring weather.

Care should be taken not to over-coddle young seedlings and to ensure they are not starved. It is not only practice and personal experience which can fully give this skill, but common sense and a close observation of the behaviour of seedlings.

Seeds should be sown in clean pots, pans or wooden

seed-boxes, and adequate drainage is necessary. Broken crocks are the best material for this purpose. If the soil can be sterilized much labour will be saved in weeding, but soil sterilization is generally a luxury the amateur gardener cannot afford, and it is not essential. A good, standard soil mixture for both sowing and pricking out is 5 parts (by bulk) of loam, 3 parts of well-rotted leaf-soil, and 3 parts of coarse sand, while to every bushel of the mixture add $1\frac{1}{2}$ ounces of superphosphate and 1 ounce of lime.

After the pots or seed-boxes have been filled the soil should be pressed down fairly firmly so that the top of

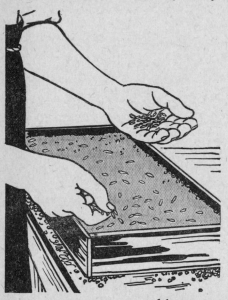

1. *Sowing seeds by broadcasting them evenly and sparingly on the surface of a seed-box. In this way the risk of over-crowding is lessened.*

the soil is about 1 inch below the edge of the receptacle. A thin layer of very fine soil should then be distributed over the surface by means of a sieve. A dusting of fine silver sand may be given before sowing, then the seeds, can be more easily seen on this and distributed more evenly. The even distribution of seeds is a matter of great importance, as at the time of germination overcrowding can be fatal to the health and future well-being of the plants.

Firming The seeds should be gently pressed into the surface with a flat, wooden presser, and then covered with very fine soil. The depth to which the seeds should be covered varies according to their size, and a good old-fashioned rule is to cover them to a depth equal to twice the thickness of an individual seed. When sowing has been completed, give the pans or boxes another gentle press so that the soil surface remains even, and water with a very fine rose. They can then be placed on the greenhouse staging or in a closed frame, and covered with newspaper. Maintain a temperature of from 50° to 55°, especially during cold, wet weather. After germination, a lower temperature is preferable. The time required for germination varies greatly. Zinnias frequently germinate in 2 or 3 days, while Antirrhinums may take 2 or 3 weeks. It is as well to keep the seed-boxes or pots covered with paper until germination takes place, as this will conserve moisture and save watering. It is essential, however, to remove the paper *immediately* the seeds germinate.

Pricking-out Once seedlings are big enough to handle,

2. Pricking out seedlings into boxes, using a tiny dibber. This should be done as soon as the seedlings are large enough to handle.

they can be pricked out into other boxes and gradually hardened off. During the first few days after pricking out, it is best to keep the boxes of seedlings shaded and with very little ventilation in order to give the young rootlets a chance to take hold of the soil. Gradually increase ventilation until the lights can be removed altogether from the frames and hardening off is completed, prior to planting out in the prepared positions. From then onwards the method of cultivation is the same as that for hardy annuals. While they are being hardened off some half-hardy annuals will benefit from being topped in order to produce bushy, robust plants. Salvias and Antirrhinums in particular respond well to this treatment, and the tops can be used as cuttings if additional plants are required.

16

If comparatively small numbers of plants are being grown, and if labour is available, better results will be obtained if certain half-hardy annuals are potted into small pots after being pricked out into boxes. These can be gradually potted on, and eventually put into the positions where they are to flower as quite large plants. Annual Carnations, bedding Calceolarias, Salpiglossis and Celosias will all give better results if treated in this way.

Avoid Starvation in the early Stages Before leaving the subject, a word of warning must be given about nourishment. During the early stages, half-hardy annuals are particularly susceptible to starvation if they are too crowded. Another dangerous time is while they are being hardened off. If unsuitable planting weather prevents the seedlings from being planted and they are left unattended for any length of time at this stage, the most serious damage will be done. In fact, all annuals must make steady and continuous growth, and they will rarely recover from a check caused by malnutrition. The easiest ways of avoiding this trouble are: do not sow too early, avoid sowing and pricking out too densely, and plant out young seedlings immediately they are ready. If, for any reason, there has to be a delay in planting out, then artificial feeding is the only remedy, and this can be given by means of liquid manure or by watering the boxes with a soluble fertilizer.

CHAPTER FOUR

ANNUALS FOR SPECIAL PURPOSES

The Cool Greenhouse Few people have facilities for growing large quantities of annuals under glass and the cultivation of such plants in pots in the cool greenhouse involves a lot of work, but it pays handsome dividends and some magnificent effects can be obtained. The remarkable exhibits of pot-grown annuals which the leading British seedsmen stage at Chelsea and other Spring Flower Shows every year are an eloquent proof of what can be done.

Seeds should be sown from August to October to provide flowering plants throughout the spring. Later sowings will, of course, prolong the flowering period. Up to the pricking-out stage the cultivation of annuals in a cool greenhouse is the same as that for the cultivation of half-hardy annuals for planting out of doors. For indoor use the young seedlings are potted either singly in small pots or, with Clarkias, Dimorphothecas, etc., several are spaced round the edge of larger pots. Immediately the pots become full of roots, plants should be repotted, and this process will have to be repeated several times until plants are finally moved into the pots in which they are to flower. These will vary in size from 5 to 12 inches, according to the type of plant.

The greatest care must be taken to ensure that the plants are not starved at any period, and applications of liquid manure will be essential. Another danger to guard against is coddling, either by keeping the temperature too high or through insufficient ventilation. To ensure the best results an entire greenhouse should be devoted to annuals, and it is not wise to try to grow them mixed up with other subjects. Much care will be necessary in watering, staking and tying. Some of the most suitable annuals for amateurs to grow as pot plants under glass are listed below. Descriptions are given in the Classified List in Chapter Six.

Alonsoa
Begonia
Calceolaria
Calendula
Campanula
Clarkia
Didiscus
Dimorphotheca
Gilia
Godetia
Hunnemannia

Impatiens
Lobelia
Mesembryanthemum
Mimulus
Nemesia
Salpiglossis
Schizanthus
Senecio
Trachelium
Venidium
Verbena

Rock Garden Quite apart from the question of ethics, there is an overwhelming argument in favour of using selected annuals in the rock garden. The judicious use of selected annuals can easily overcome the flowerless period of late summer, and so make the rock garden attractive for a much longer period, although the true alpine enthusiast will tell you that, provided a proper choice of alpines is made, this flowerless period need never occur.

Hardy annuals are most suited for the rock garden, as they can be sown where they are to flower and may be sown in any odd place where there is room. Some will, in time, become naturalized and seed themselves in almost inaccessible positions in rock crevices. As there is less digging and weeding in a rock garden than in open ground, the chances of self-sown seedlings appearing are greater. Some of the most suitable and less common annuals for growing in the rock garden are mentioned below. Detailed descriptions are given in the Classified List in Chapter Six.

Aethionema graecum
Alyssum maritimum vars.
Calceolaria chelidonioides
Chrysanthemum Mawii
Dianthus
Dimorphothecas (dwarf)
Eschscholzia tenuifolia
Felicia
Linaria
Mesembryanthemum
Nemophila maculata
Phacelia campanularia
Portulacas, single and double
Ursinia
Zinnia Haageana

Climbers   As climbers annuals have a particular value for they produce quick results for screening or where pergolas and trellis-work need temporary cover. The variety of plants which can be grown as climbing annuals is greater than often realized, and the following list gives the most noteworthy. They are best grown from seeds sown in small pots, and planted out when 6 to 10 inches high, as such plants will be robust enough to take hold immediately of whatever support they are going to climb on. To provide initial support small sticks can be placed in the pots, and these can be left in position when planting is done.

Sweet Peas, of course, take pride of place as climbing

annuals, although they have the disadvantage of requiring specially prepared positions and are not suitable for places where there is only a restricted amount of soil, such as in tubs, etc.

Probably the easiest to grow of all annual climbers is the ever popular *Ipomoea purpurea* (*Convolvulus major*) the Morning Glory, which, with its rich purple or crimson flowers and attractive leaves never fails to produce excellent results. A less common and even more beautiful convolvulus is *Ipomoea tricolor* (syn. *I. rubro-caerula*), with blooms 4 inches in diameter and clear, sky-blue in colour, while an equally large, carmine-coloured, Continental variety is called *Meraviglia scarlatto*.

It should be stressed that these are not perennial in this country. They are killed by the first frosts and are not pernicious perennial weeds like the native convolvulus or bindweed, and should not be confused with it.

Although sometimes despised as being too common, Nasturtiums are still the ideal climbing annual for almost any position. They are fast growing, have attractive foliage (which is edible) and most handsome flowers. Another very lovely climber is the Canary Creeper (*Tropaeolum peregrinum*), with its quaintly segmented yellow flowers. *Quamoclit lobata* or *Mina lobata*, as it is sometimes listed in seed catalogues, should be more widely grown, as its curious little blooms are a mixture of red, yellow and orange and always attract much attention.

Another uncommon climber is *Cobaea scandens* which, while it is perennial under favourable conditions, is ideal for growing as an annual. The Maurandyas are all of very great beauty, especially *Maurandya Barclaiana* and *M. scandens*. All of these, together with Humulus, Eccremocarpus and Vicias, are described more fully in the Classified List in Chapter Six.

Window-boxes, Brackets and Hanging Baskets The annuals used for these purposes should be of compact, semi-dwarf habit or have a tendency to hang or trail. Window-boxes must have adequate drainage provided, and if made of wood should have a metal lining. Baskets and brackets are best lined with live moss before being filled with soil. The type of soil can be similar to that used for pricking out seedlings or soilless culture methods can be employed and the plants grown in vermiculite. They are fed with a proprietary nutrient solution supplied, with full instructions for use, with the bags of vermiculite. Small, pot-grown plants are the most suitable for furnishing boxes and baskets. During hot or windy weather constant watering will be necessary, and applications of liquid manure will be advantageous. The following is a selection of plants which may be grown as annuals, and are suitable for window-box or basket cultivation. Descriptions are given in the Classified List in Chapter Six.

Ageratum
Antirrhinum (dwarf)
Aster (dwarf)
Begonia
Celosia
Eschscholzia

Linaria
Lobelia
Mesembryanthemum
Nemesia
Petunia
Phlox Drummondii

Reseda   Ursinia
Salvia   Verbena
Tropaeolum (dwarf)

Everlasting Flowers When the summer display has finished some annuals continue to provide welcome colour indoors throughout the winter. These are the so-called 'Everlasting Flowers', whose petals retain their colouring and do not fall even when dead. A selection of these should be grown in every garden, as even if they are not appreciated for drying they are still first-rate annuals for the garden. These Everlasting Flowers are all easy to grow, and require the same treatment as other annuals, except that they are devout sun lovers and more tolerant of drought. They are usually more successful during a hot, dry summer than in a cold, wet season.

When gathering the blooms it is essential to choose a dry, sunny day, and cut the flowers when they are fully expanded. Tie them into bunches and hang them in a dry, well-ventilated place for a few days until any remaining moisture has evaporated. The flowers can then be either stored or arranged in vases without water. They will require dusting during winter, and this is best done with a small pair of bellows. Some pleasing effects can be obtained by combining such flowers with dried grasses or the dried seed-heads of such annuals as Love-in-a-Mist, Poppies and Honesty. These latter can also be sprayed with paint to make them even more attractive.

There are quite a lot of these Everlasting Flowers to choose from, but Helichrysum and Statice are the most popular. All of the following are worth growing, and

23

descriptions are given in the Classified List in Chapter Six.

Acroclinium (*see* Helipterum)	Helipterum
Ammobium	Waitzia
Catananche caerulea	Xeranthemum
Gomphrena	

Annuals for Naturalizing It is not generally appreciated that annuals are ideal plants for naturalizing or broadcast sowing. This is often how they grow in their natural habitat, and by using this method some striking effects can be achieved at very little cost, an item of some consequence these days. Obviously it is not practicable to naturalize in a very small garden, but such sites as a paddock, the edge of a wood, banks of a stream or pond, and any area of rough grassland are ideal; while as a temporary measure whole areas of a moderately sized garden could be treated in such a way. I have sometimes seen the method employed in public parks, when turf has been removed for using in other places, and instead of leaving the position bare, annuals have been sown broadcast. Considerable quantities of seed are necessary for such work, and home-gathered seed is of particular value for this purpose. (See also Chaper Five.)

The preparation of the site is an easy matter. Grass, turf, coarse weeds, etc., should be removed and the land well dug or ploughed in autumn, during the winter or very early spring. If some manure or rotted leaf-soil can be spread over the site before digging, this will be an advantage. In March or April rake the ground to obtain as fine a surface as possible, and then sow the chosen seed broadcast, by hand. Under such conditions thinning out will not be necessary or even possible, so seeds should be sown more thinly than is usual. An excellent way to ensure thin sowing and even spacing is to mix the seed with double the amount of dry sand, and then scatter this mixture over the site. Seeds can be covered by raking them into the surface. When big areas are treated in this way, weeding will not be practicable, and it will be sufficient to remove any big, coarse weeds, such as docks and nettles. Some of these can be dealt with by using selective weed-killers.

The most suitable annuals for naturalizing are Asters, Eschscholzias, Marigolds, Petunias and Poppies.

ANNUALS FOR SPECIAL POSITIONS

Annuals suitable for various situations are listed below, and each of the plants mentioned is described in detail in the Classified List in Chapter Six.

Edges

Ageratum Houstonianum (dwarf vars.)

Alonsoa Warscewiczii var. *compactum*

Alyssum maritimum

Antirrhinum (Tom Thumb vars.)

Cheiranthus Allionii

Iberis umbellata (dwarf vars.)

Lobelia Erinus

Mesembryanthemum criniflorum

Nemophila maculata

Ursinia anthemoides

Ursinia pulchra

Verbena venosa (syn. *V. rigida*)

Viola tricolor hybrids

Zinnia Haageana

Zinnia linearis

25

Backgrounds

Helianthus annuus
Helianthus argophyllus
Lavatera trimestris

Ricinus communis
Zea Mays

Dot Plants

Amaranthus caudatus
Amaranthus Henderi
Amaranthus salicifolius
Cleome spinosa

Kochia scoparia trichophila
Ricinus communis
Zea Mays

Massing

Alonsoa Warscewiczii
Antirrhinum (bedding and Tom Thumb vars.)
Aster chinensis
Aster (Ostrich Plume, Comet, Chrysanthemum flowered and dwarf vars.)
Calendula officinalis vars.
Clarkia pulchella vars.
Cleome spinosa
Coreopsis tinctoria
Coreopsis Drummondii
Dahlia (Coltness Gem hybrids)
Dimorphotheca aurantiaca hybrids
Dimorphotheca Ecklonis
Dimorphotheca pluvialis
Emilia sagittata (syn. *E. flammea*)
Eschscholzia californica

Gazania splendens
Godetia amoena
Godetia grandiflora
Impatiens Balsamina
Linaria Broussonetii
Linaria maroccana
Lobelia cardinalis
Lobelia siphilitica
Lobelia siphilitica var. *alba*
Nemesia strumosa
Petunia, single bedding
Phlox Drummondii
Tagetes erecta
Tagetes patula
Tagetes signata
Ursinia anethoides
Ursinia pulchra
Verbena hybrida
Verbena venosa
Zinnia Haageana
Zinnia linearis

Blue Border

Ageratum Houstonianum
Aster (blue vars. of any annual forms)
Centaurea Cyanus
Dracocephalum Moldavica
Felicia Bergeriana
Felicia rotundifolia
Lobelia Erinus
Lobelia siphilitica
Lobelia vedrariensis
Nemesia strumosa (blue vars.)
Nemophila Menziesii
Nigella damascena
Nigella hispanica
Nolana lanceolata
Petunia hybrids (such as var. Blue Bedder)
Phacelia campanularia
Verbena hybrids (blue vars.)

Semi-shade

Campanula Medium (annual form)
Dracocephalum Moldavica
Impatiens Balsamina
Impatiens Roylei
Lobelia Erinus
Lobelia siphilitica
Mimulus brevipes
Mimulus luteus
Mimulus moschatus
Nemophila maculata
Nemophila Menziesii
Oenothera acaulis
Oenothera biennis
Oenothera missouriensis
Salvia splendens
Viola tricolor hybrids

Carpet Bedding

Ageratum Houstonianum (dwarf form)
Alyssum maritimum var. Little Dorrit
Alyssum maritimum var. Violet Queen
Felicia Bergeriana
Gilia dianthoides
Iberis umbellata (dwarf vars.)
Lobelia Erinus
Mimulus moschatus
Nemophila maculata
Nemophila Menziesii
Portulaca grandiflora
Verbena hybrids
Verbena venosa

CHAPTER FIVE

SAVING YOUR OWN SEED

THE fact that most annuals are raised from seed (a few can be propagated from cuttings) adds a greater significance and value to seed collecting. Practically every annual produces a rich harvest of seed, and collecting, drying and storing it can be instructive and interesting. Purity of strain will be lost from home-collected seeds, while novelties and new varieties must of course be purchased from the seedsman. When large quantities are required and individual colours are not an essential, the home-saved seed will generally give excellent results.

The equipment necessary is a good supply of stout paper-bags, a pencil, basket and scissors. The seeds should be ripe at the time of collection, and should be gathered on a fine day. If collected before they are fully matured, seeds will give poor germination, and if collection is delayed too long only empty seed-vessels will be found. Annuals are perhaps the easiest of all seeds to collect as they are generally produced in large quantities, and often the almost dry flower-head can be collected.

When there are seeds ready for collection, the name should be written on an empty paper-bag, and the seed either picked or cut from the plant and placed in the bag for transfer to the place where the seeds are to dry. Sometimes there will be pods, sometimes bunches, and sometimes berries or individual seeds. Almost any light, airy room or shed is suitable for drying and storing seeds, provided there is space for tables or shelves and plenty of ventilation. Ventilation is of great importance as it is so easy for seeds to go mouldy, especially in autumn when most seed collecting is done. Empty the contents of the paper-bags into cardboard boxes, and in each box place a label bearing the name of the seed. I have always found it unwise to try to dry seeds in metal or earthenware receptacles, as these are not absorbent and the seeds are slow to dry. The boxes can be left until seeds are ready for cleaning, but it is advisable to disturb the contents now and again so that air penetrates.

Seed cleaning presents its own problems. Leguminous plants such as Lathyrus and Lupins are easy, while members of the poppy family require a gentle shake for the ripe seeds to fall out of the capsules, already cleaned. Some are exasperating to clean, especially those which are sticky, have spines or fly all over the place as soon as touched. I find that the most useful tools for helping with seed cleaning are small sieves, with a wide range of meshes. By passing the seeds from one to the other many can be separated from the chaff. Digitalis, Petunias, Antirrhinums, etc., can all be dealt with in this way; while larger seeds, such as Zinnias, are best cleaned by hand. Many seeds can be cleaned by just shaking them about in a closed paper-bag.

Dry, cleaned seeds are best stored in small glass jars (without lids) labelled and arranged in alphabetical order on shelves in an open cupboard in a medium temperature.

CHAPTER SIX

CLASSIFIED LIST

HA = hardy annual. HHA = half-hardy annual.
B = biennial. P = perennial. ft. = feet. in. = inches.

The biennials and perennials included in this list can conveniently be grown as annuals.

Abronia (Sand Verbena) (P) Trailing plants suitable for rock garden, window-boxes, baskets or borders. Sweetly scented flowers similar to Verbena. Sow in open ground in April or under glass in March. *A. Bigelowii,* white, June–July, 9 in.; *A. latifolia* (syn. *A. arenaria*), yellow, July, 1 ft.; *A. umbellata,* pink, June–July, 1 ft.

Acroclinium, *see* Helipterum.

Adonis (Pheasant's Eye) (HA) Finely cut foliage and free flowering. Useful for mixed border if grown in quantity. Can be grown in half-shade. Sow in open ground in March. *A. aestivalis,* crimson, June–July, 1 ft.; *A. autumnalis* (syn. *A. annua*), scarlet, July–September, 1–1½ ft.

Aethionema (Stone Cress) (P) Attractive dwarf plants ideal for rock garden or edging. Require a dry, sunny position. Treat as HHA and sow under glass in March–April. *A. cappadocicum* (syn. *Thlaspi arabicum*), pale pink, June, 6 in.; *A. graecum,* rarely offered for sale, but a first-class plant which deserves a place of honour as an alpine or border subject. Masses of bright pink flowers for many months throughout the summer. Will withstand even the worst weather. Glaucous green foliage. Naturalizes freely, 2–3 in.

African Marigold, *see* Tagetes erecta.

Agathaea, *see* Felicia.

Ageratum (Floss Flower) (HHA)   The many dwarf varieties are among the most useful of all annuals for bedding, edging and carpeting. They are easy to grow, and flower throughout the summer. Sow under glass March–April. *A. Houstonianum* (syn. *A. mexicanum*), blue, June–October, 1–2 ft. Dwarf varieties: Blue Ball, Fairy Pink, Imperial White, all 6 in.

Alonsoa (Mask Flower) (P)   Vividly coloured, worthy of wider cultivation. Prefer rich soil in sunny position. Treat as HHA. Excellent for massing. Sow under glass in March, plant out young pot-grown plants in May. *A. Warscewiczii*, scarlet flowers throughout summer if occasionally cut back, 1½–2 ft. The variety *compacta* is a dwarf form useful for the cool greenhouse.

Alyssum (Madwort) (HA *or* P)   One of the most easily grown and useful of all dwarf annuals for edging, bedding and as a groundwork. Also suitable for rock gardens and window-boxes. Sow under glass in March or outside in April. Flowers scented. *A. maritimum* (Sweet Alyssum), white, blooms throughout the summer, 6–12 in. The following are excellent varieties: Little Dorrit, white, dwarf, bushy plants, 4 in. ; *procumbens*, white, low, spreading habit; Violet Queen, a truly remarkable plant with a flowering period of many months, bright violet, 4 in. The perennial Alyssums, such as the yellow-

flowered *A. saxatile,* can also be flowered the first year
from seed, but should be sown early under glass.

Amaranthus (HHA) Valuable as foliage plants as well
as for their curious inflorescences. Those with coloured
leaves are particularly useful as pot plants for the greenhouse. Sow under glass in April, plant out in June in full
sun, avoid over-watering. *A. caudatus* (Love-lies-bleeding), 2–3 ft. Pale green leaves, blood-red flowers in the
form of a long catkin often 2 ft. in length. Can be sown
in the open ground but will require drastic thinning out.
A. gangeticus varieties, crimson, yellow, green or mottled
leaves, inconspicuous flowers, valuable for bedding,
1–3 ft. *A. Henderi,* a hybrid, rosy-carmine leaves, 2–3 ft.
A. salicifolius (Fountain Plant), elegant species, long,
drooping leaves, bronze-green to orange, 2–3 ft.

Ammobium (HHA) Easily grown 'Everlasting Flowers'.
Sow in April in open ground. *A. alatum* var. *grandiflorum,*
white with yellow centre, dried flowers last well, 2½ ft.

Anagallis (Pimpernel) (HA *and* P) Attractive, low-grow-
ing plants ideal for rock garden and edge of borders.
Useful for pots and baskets. Sow under glass in March
or in open ground in April. *A. linifolia* (syn. *A. grandiflora*), blue, July–August, 6–9 in. Varieties: *carnea,* pink;
coccinea, red.

Antirrhinum (Snapdragon) (P) One of the most popular
and attractive of all plants grown annually for bedding
and cut bloom. All good seedsmen list a great many
types of all colours, ranging in height from 6 in. to 3 ft.
Flowers throughout the summer if dead blooms are removed. Treat as HHA and sow under glass in late Feb-

ruary or early March. The various types are as follows:

Tall, 3 ft.   Intermediate, 1½ ft.
Bedding, 9 in.   Tom Thumb, 6 in.

Rock Hybrids, almost prostrate, excellent for
    carpeting and the rock garden.

For names and descriptions of individual varieties see
seedsmen's catalogues. In certain districts Antirrhinums
are difficult to grow because of rust disease, and during
recent years much experimental work has been carried
out to obtain a strain which is rust resistant. Most seedsmen now offer a selection of such varieties which can be
grown with safety. There is not yet a wide colour range.

Apple of Peru, *see* Nicandra.

Arctotis (HHA) South African plants of great beauty.
Must have light, well-drained soil and plenty of sun.
Easy to grow if planted out in April or May from seeds
sown under glass in March. Long flowering period,
brilliant, daisy-like blooms. *A. stoechadifolia grandis,*
white with blue centre, 1½ ft. *A hybrida,* a strain known
as 'Sutton's hybrids' has been introduced and includes
white, yellow, orange, red and crimson flowered forms,
9 in. *A. speciosa* (syn. *A. acaulis*), orange with red on
reverse of petals, 1½ ft.

Argemone (Prickly Poppy) (HA) Unjustifiably neglected,
very beautiful plant. Large, poppy-like flowers and handsome, spiny, thistle-like leaves. Big prickly seed-pods.
Sow in open ground in April. Light soil, sunny position.
Flowers throughout the summer. *A. mexicana,* yellow,
2 ft. A weed in many tropical countries, and a hundred

and fifty years ago could be found growing wild in London. Var. *ochroleuca,* yellowish-white, 2 ft.; *A. platyceras,* white, 2 ft.

Arnebia (HHA) Easily grown but not generally popular. Marigold-like flowers. Sow under glass in March. *A.*

3. A r n e b i a cornuta. *Easily grown, free-flowering plants, but not often seen in the average garden. The yellow and black flowers are like miniature Marigolds.*

cornuta, yellow flowers spotted black, summer, 2 ft.

Artemisia (P) Often cultivated because of its rapid growth and handsome foliage. Makes a pleasing contrast as a dot plant in beds of brightly coloured flowers, because of its pyramidal growth. Sow under glass in March and plant out in May. *A. sacrorum viride,* finely cut, fragrant, fern-like foliage, up to 4 ft. Closely related to the shrubby 'Old Man' (*Artemisia Abrotanum*).

Asperula (Woodruff) (HA) Very easily grown and ideal for using as a groundwork among shrubs or for edging. Sow in open in April. *A. orientalis*, sky-blue, scented, June–August, 10 in.

Aster (By some authorities Annual Asters are now called Callistephus) (HHA) Annual asters are probably the most valuable of all plants for a long summer display and for cut bloom. There is now a vast number of types and forms, ranging through a wide selection of colours. Easy to grow although sometimes a virus disease known as wilt will cause trouble and once ground has become contaminated asters should not be grown there again for several years. The best preventives are: reliable seed, not too much artificial heat in the young stage and generally good cultivation. Sow in gentle heat at the beginning of April or in cold frames in May. The principal forms are:

Single-flowered Southcote Beauty, mid-season, white, pink, scarlet, mauve, purple, 2–2½ ft.

   Chinensis. Mid-season, ideal for cutting. Crimson, mauve, dark blue, purple, white, pink, 2 ft.

Double-flowered Ostrich Plume. Loose feathery flowers, fine for cutting. Mid-season, very wide range of colours, 18 in.

   Comet. Flowers resemble Japanese-chrysanthemums. Mid-season, white, pink, blue, 18 in.

   Mammoth. Very long flowers on long stems, late flowering, many colours, 2½–3 ft.

Californian Giant. Enormous blooms, latest of all to flower, many colours, 2–3 ft.

Chrysanthemum Flowered Tall. Very double flowers, mid-season, many colours, 1½ ft.

Chrysanthemum Flowered Dwarf. Ideal for massing, mid-season, many colours, 9 in.

Miniature Pompon. Button-like flowers, mid-season, various colours, 12 in.

Peony Flowered. Big, incurved blooms, mid-season, various colours, 2 ft.

Atriplex (Salt Bush) (HA) Large-growing plant with spinach-like leaves which make it attractive for growing as a foliage plant. Sow out of doors in April. *A. hortensis atrosanguinea*. Crimson leaves, likes rich soil, 4 ft.

Australian Everlasting Flower, *see* Helipterum.

Baby Blue-eyes, *see* Nemophila Menziesii.

Balsam, *see* Impatiens.

Bartonia, *see* Mentzelia.

Beard Tongue, *see* Penstemon.

Begonia Although really half-hardy perennials, the fibrous rooted begonias are first-class plants for growing as half-hardy annuals, both as pot plants and for bedding. As plants are slow growing during their early stages, seeds should be sown in heat not later than February to ensure plants for bedding out in June. Well-grown plants will provide an abundance of small but showy flowers for a long period, and are especially suitable for massing. *B. gracilis* and its hybrids are about 6 in. high; Fireball, crimson; Pink Profusion, pink; *luminosa*, scarlet; White Pearl, etc. *B. semperflorens*

36

hybrids and crosses are from 6 to 15 in. high, and include Bedding Queen, rose-pink, 12–15 in.; Salmon Queen, red, 12–15 in.; White Queen, 12–15 in.

Bell Flower, *see* Campanula.

Bellis (Daisy) (P) Although common, these large, double-flowered forms of the common daisy (*B. perennis*) are of great value as annuals. They are easy to grow, free-flowering and bloom very early. Sow in cold frames in February or during late summer for earliest results in spring. *B. perennis* var. Longfellow, deep rose; var. Snowball, white; var. Quilled Etna, red.

Bellium (False Daisy) (P) Several small-flowered daisy-like plants well suited to the rock garden because of their trailing habit. To flower the same year sow under glass in March. *B. bellidioides,* white flowers, 3 in.; *B. minutum,* very tiny blooms, lilac, 3 in.

Bindweed, *see* Ipomoea.

Black-eyed Susan, *see* Rudbeckia and Thunbergia.

Blue Lace Flower, *see* Trachymene.

Brachycome (Swan River Daisy) (HHA) A remarkably beautiful annual. Requires a dry, sunny position. Very long flowering period. Sow under glass in late March. *B. iberidifolia alba,* white; var. Blue Gem, blue and white; var. Mauve Beauty, mauve. All 1–1½ ft.

Browallia (HHA) Chiefly suitable as pot plants for the greenhouse. All delightful shades of blue. Sow indoors in March. *B. americana,* the most suitable species for outdoor culture, violet-blue, 1 ft.; *B. speciosa* var. *major,* best grown as a pot plant, violet-blue, July, 1–2 ft.

Butterfly Flower, *see* Schizanthus.

Calandrinia (Rock Purslane) (HA *or* P)   Dwarf or semi-trailing plants suitable for edging or the rock garden. Sow under glass in March or out of doors in April. Require a dry, sunny position. *C. grandiflora,* rosy-purple, poppy-like flowers in mid-summer, light green, fleshy leaves, 1 ft.; *C. umbellata,* striking, vivid magenta-coloured flowers all summer, trailing habit, 4–6 in.

Calceolaria (Slipper Flower) (HHA *or* P)   As a pot-grown plant for the greenhouse the calceolaria has few rivals. If sown in July and grown on throughout the winter large plants will be available for flowering in early spring. Several species are also excellent for bedding. *C. chelidonioides,* small yellow flowers, suitable for bedding. Sow under glass in March, 1–1½ ft. *C. herbeo-hybrida,* and its varieties are the most suitable for pot culture. Most seedsmen offer a wide range of colours. Not to be recommended for bedding purposes as their large, heavy trusses of bloom do not stand up well to bad weather. *C. mexicana,* a showy, annual, yellow-flowered species for bedding, 1 ft. *C. scabiosaefolia,* another very attractive yellow-flowered species with hairy leaves. Particularly effective in bold masses and tolerates semi-shade, 1½ ft.

Calendula (Marigold) (HA)   The fact that calendulas have been so widely grown for so many years is eloquent proof of their value as annual bedders. Instead of becoming less popular they are now more widely grown than ever, and many new varieties have been introduced ranging through orange, lemon, cream and apricot. Easy to grow, not particular about soil, they flower throughout the summer and are valuable for cutting. Sow in open ground from March onwards. Can also be sown in autumn if earlier flowering plants are required. *C. officinalis* (Pot Marigold), the true species, grows to about 2 ft. and is not particularly attractive, but modern varieties such as Orange King, Lemon Queen, Radio, Twilight, *chrysantha*, etc., are excellent.

Californian Poppy, *see* Eschscholzia.

Callirhoë (Poppy Mallow) (HA *and* P) Not often seen, but these are delightful plants and easy to grow. Sow under glass in March. Prefer light soil and sun. *C. digitata*, magenta-coloured flowers similar to a poppy, 2½ ft.; *C. involucrata*, trailing species, large crimson flowers, mid-summer; *C. pedata*, can be sown in open ground April, red flowers with white eye, 1½ ft.

Callistephus, *see* Aster.

Campanula (Bellflower) (P, B *or* HA) There are few true annual campanulas, but those which do exist are of considerable garden value. A noteworthy and fairly new addition is the annual form of the normally biennial canterbury bell (*C. medium*), which should be sown under glass in March. All other annual campanulas can be sown out of doors in April. *C. Cecilii*, large, lavender-blue flowers, excellent for pot culture, 1½ ft.; *C. drabifolia*, ideal for edging or rock garden, violet-blue, July, 4 in.; *C. medium* (annual form), pink or blue, mid-summer, 1½ ft.; *C. sulphurea*, pale yellow flowers and grey foliage, best sown under glass in March, 9 in.

Campion, *see* Lychnis.

Canary Creeper, *see* Tropaeolum peregrinum.

Candytuft, *see* Iberis.

Canna (P) Generally grown from tubers, which have to be lifted and dried in autumn like Dahlias. With a little trouble can also be raised from seed. If sown in heat in February will be ready for planting out in May, and flower throughout the late summer and autumn. Before sowing, seeds should be soaked in water for 24 hours and slightly notched with a small file. Rich soil and full sun is essential. *C. indica* hybrids, flowers red, yellow, orange or pink, large handsome leaves, either green or dark red, 3–5 ft. The flowering period will be prolonged if dead flowers are regularly removed.

Cannabis (Hemp) (HA) Of no great attraction as flowering plants, a few of economic value greatly add to the interest of any garden. The foliage is quite attractive and useful for filling odd spaces in borders or the wild garden. *C. sativa*, sow in open ground March–April, vigorous plants will reach a height of 6–8 ft.

Canterbury Bell (annual), *see* Campanula medium.

Cape Marigold, *see* Dimorphotheca.

Carnation (annual), *see* Dianthus.

Castor Oil Plant, *see* Ricinus communis.

Catananche (P) Elegant border plants. Sow under glass in March. Flowers can be dried for winter. *C. caerulea*, violet-blue flowers on long stems, excellent for cutting, July–August, 2 ft. There is also a yellow form, var. *lutea*.

Catchfly, *see* Silene.

Celosia (Cockscomb) (HHA) Highly decorative for the cool greenhouse. There are two forms, crested and feathered, brilliant shades of orange, yellow and red. Remain in flower for a long period. Rich soil and con-

4. Catananche caerulea. *Graceful, violet-blue flowers of considerable value for cutting. An excellent subject for the mixed border.*

stant feeding during the growing period is essential if the best results are to be obtained. Can reach a height of from 2–3 ft. Sow in heat in March. Can also be bedded out in June or July from pot-grown plants. *C. argentea* var. *cristata,* there are many seedsmen's hybrids and forms of these Crested Celosias; *C. argentea* var. *plumosa,* handsome forms with silky plumes instead of crests.

Centaurea (Cornflower, Sweet Sultan) (HA *or* P) Well-known plants of great beauty for their delightful colours and attractive foliage. Invaluable for cutting and for growing in mixed borders throughout the summer. Sow in open ground in April. In districts where winters are not too vigorous they can also be sown out of doors in autumn, to produce earlier flowering plants in spring. *C. Cineraria* (syn. *C. ratifolia*), grown for its beautiful, silvery leaves which are effective when used for bedding; *C. Clementei,* a useful foliage plant with a white, woolly appearance, pale yellow, 3 ft.; *C. Cyanus* (cornflower), originally only obtainable in blue, but now available in pink and white as well, and should be included in every mixed border, 3 ft.; there is also a dwarf form, 1 ft.; *C. moschata* (Sweet Sultan), among the most effective of all summer annuals, but essentially a fine-weather plant. It is, however, so prized for its beauty and value as cut blooms that a little extra care is well worth while in its culture. Purple, white, mauve and yellow varieties, 1½ ft.

Centranthus (Valerian) (P) Easily grown and attractive plants which can often be naturalized in steps, walls and among rocks to achieve some delightful effects. They are really perennials, but can be raised and flowered as annuals. Sow outside in April. *C. macrosiphon,* pink, July–August, good for massing, 1½ ft.; the var. *alba* is a white form; *C. ruber,* red, very free flowering throughout the summer, 1½–2 ft.; vars. *atrococcineus,* red, *alba,* white.

Cheiranthus (Wallflower) (P) Mostly perennials, but one fine hybrid can be cultivated as an annual if sown in the open in summer, so that good-sized plants can be bedded out the following spring. *C. Allionii,* vivid, orange flowers which make a brilliant display in late spring and summer if grown in masses, 1 ft. Commonly known as 'Siberian Wallflower'.

Cherry Pie, *see* Heliotropium peruvianum.

Chilean Bell Flower, *see* Nolana.

Chilean Glory Flower, *see* Eccremocarpus scaber.

Chrysanthemum (P *or* HA) The annual chrysanthemums are indispensable for a successful display of summer-flowering annuals. There are many brilliantly coloured varieties, easy to grow, and the flowers are excellent for cutting. Sow in open ground in April or under glass in March. The many hybrids offered in seedmen's catalogues are varieties of the following three species: *C. carinatum, C. segetum* (Corn Marigold) and *C. coronarium*). There are single and double forms, yellow, white, brown, bronze, scarlet and orange; mostly with contrasting coloured eyes or markings, 1–2 ft. Effective displays can also be obtained by sowing a mixture of all three kinds. *C. frutescens* (Marguerite), one of the most popular of all greenhouse plants, this lovely white marguerite is grown in enormous quantities for the flower markets. Sow in February and repeatedly pot on for indoor work or bed out in May, 2–3 ft. A lovely pale yellow form is var. Comtesse de Chambord. *C. Mawii,* finely cut silver leaves and tiny, single pink flowers, 6–12 in. A lovely little species of compact growth, ideal for the rock garden. Sow under glass in February and plant out pot-grown plants in May.

Cineraria, *see* Senecio cruentus.

Clarkia (HA) One of the easiest to grow of all annuals, and yet one of the most effective. There is a very wide range of colours and almost any kind of soil or weather is suitable. Sow out of doors in April or under glass in

March. Can also be grown as pot plants for indoors if sown in September, when they can reach a height of 5 ft. and flower in spring. Both indoor and outdoor grown plants require support as they are liable to be top heavy, especially in wind. *C. elegans,* many magnificent garden varieties with either single or double flowers, colours range from white to purple and from pink to scarlet, bloom throughout the summer, excellent for cutting, 2 ft.; *C. pulchella* and varieties, dwarfer, ideal for edges and borders, mauve, white, pink, 1–1½ ft.

Cleome (Spider Flower) (HHA) A most beautiful and curious plant. The common name well describes the handsome flowers, which have conspicuous stamens,

5. C l e o m e spinosa (*Spider Flower*). *An un-common and beautiful annual, with curious seed-pods which are produced while the plant is still bearing its pinkish - mauve flowers.*

pinkish-mauve in colour and 4 or 5 in. long. It seems to be rarely cultivated in private gardens, but is greatly admired whenever seen. The long, thin seed vessels are also decorative, while the spiny foliage is most attractive. Sow under glass in March and plant out in May, prefer-

6. Cobaea scandens (*Cups and Saucers*). *A beautiful, fast-growing climber, suitable for trellis or pergola. Large, creamy-white and violet blooms.*

ably from small pots. If well grown each plant will occupy more than one square yard of space. *C. spinosa* hybrids, flowers vary from pale pink to mauve, 5 ft.

Cobaea (Cups and Saucers) (HHA *or* P) A handsome, fast-growing climber suitable for the cool greenhouse or outside use on pergolas and trellis. Sow under glass in March, and plant out young, pot-grown plants in late

May or June. Prefer warm, sunny position in rich soil. *C. scandens,* large flowers, 1½ in. in diameter, similar to single bloom of Canterbury Bell, bloom in late summer. Flowers in the young stage are creamy-white, and turn to a deep violet colour after a few days. The large, egg-shaped seed-pods are also attractive, 10–30 ft.

Cockscomb, *see* Celosia.

Collinsia (HA) Dwarf growing, very free flowering and easy to cultivate. Sow out of doors in April. *C. bicolor,* lilac and white, summer, 1 ft.; *C. grandiflora,* showy blue and white flowers, June–July, 1 ft.; var. *carminea,* purple.

Collomia (HA, B *or* P) Very hardy and easy to raise. Dwarf and free flowering with brilliant colours. Sow in March or April in open ground. *C. coccinea,* vivid scarlet flowers, June, 1½ ft.; *C. grandiflora,* salmon blooms, 1½ ft.

Convolvulus (Bindweed), *see* Ipomoea.

Coreopsis (HA *or* P) Magnificent, free-flowering plants for border or massing, and excellent for cut bloom. Easy to grow in all types of soil. Sow in open ground March or April. *C. atrosanguinea,* dark red flowers, mid-summer, 3 ft.; *C. Drummondii,* golden-yellow flowers with reddish-brown centre, summer, 1½ ft.; *C. tinctoria,* yellow and brown, summer, 2 ft.; var. *nana compacta* is bright yellow with dark crimson eye, 8 in.

Cornflower, *see* Centaurea Cyanus.

Cosmos (HHA) Cosmos are easily grown annuals which seem to possess all the virtues of a good plant. The foliage is feathery and attractive; the graceful flowers are borne on long, slender stalks and have a wide range of delicate colours. Single and semi-double forms flower

46

7. Cosmos sul-phureus. *An ideal plant for bedding as its freely produced, golden - orange coloured blooms remain in flower for many months.*

from late spring until early autumn, and there are varia-tions in height from 2–5 ft. The taller forms are excellent for mixed borders, while the dwarfs are ideal for massing in beds. Sow earliest varieties under glass in March and plant out in May. Sow in open ground April or May. *C. bipinnatus,* large single flowers, lilac-purple, August, 4–5 ft. There are many forms and separate colours offered in seedmen's catalogues. *C. sulphureus,* comparatively small flowers, golden-orange, 2½ ft. Very fine for bedding.

Cotula (HA *or* P) Dwarf, creeping plants ideal for the rock garden, edging, baskets and window-boxes. Prefer full sun but will tolerate the poorest soils. Sow under glass in March or April. *C. barbata,* yellow flowers, 6 in.

Cream Cups, *see* Platystemon californicus.

Cuphea (HHA *or* P) Lovely evergreen plants for pot cultivation under glass, but also used as a summer bedding plant if the weather is warm and dry. Sow under glass in March. *C. platycentra* (syn. *C. ignea*), scarlet tubular flowers tipped with black, July, 1 ft.

Cups and Saucers, *see* Cobaea scandens.

Dahlia (P) The only Dahlias which are really worth growing from seed are the so-called Coltness Gem Hybrids. Most of the other types can be raised from seed, but more satisfactory results will be obtained by growing them from tubers or young plants raised from cuttings. The Coltness Gem Hybrids give excellent results from seed if sown in gentle heat in March, the seedlings potted on and planted out in May or June. They are obtainable as a mixture or in separate colours, such as scarlet, orange, yellow or white, $1\frac{1}{2}$–2 ft. Flowering period from mid-summer until the first frost. Dahlias raised from seed will produce fine young tubers which can be lifted, stored, and planted again the following year.

Daisy, *see* Bellis.

Datura (Trumpet Flower) (HHA *or* P) Two annual daturas are worth growing from seed for the sake of their handsome foliage, attractive, trumpet-shaped flowers and curious, spiny seed-pods. Sow in heat in March, grow on in small pots and plant out when all danger of frost is over. They require rich soil, full sun and plenty of space.

D. meteloides, blue and white, mid-summer until autumn, 2–3 ft.; *D. Stramonium* (Thorn Apple), white, 2 ft.

Delphinium (including Larkspur) (HA *or* P)   Although really perennials, varieties of *Delphinium grandiflorum* can easily be raised from seed and treated as annuals. They are, in fact, some of the most attractive of all plants suitable for bedding, and are also of great value for cutting. Sow under glass in early March or in open ground in April. There are various shades of white and blue. Cultivation is easy and the flowering period long, but a sunny open position is essential. *D. grandiflorum* hybrids, a number of dwarf varieties such as Azure Fairy, Blue Butterfly, Blue Gem, etc., are offered by most seedsmen,

8. Dianthus chinensis *hybrids (Japanese Pinks). A magnificent strain of dwarf-growing Pinks with a remarkable range of richly coloured flowers.*

mid-summer, 1–2 ft.; *D. grandiflorum* var. *paniculatum* has finely cut foliage and small, violet-blue flowers, 1 ft.; *D. Ajacis* (Larkspur) is a true annual delphinium and one of our most lovely bedding plants.

Dianthus (Carnation, Pink) (HA, HHA *and* P) Few people seem to realize the full value of annual carnations. Beautiful, double flowers can be produced within six months of sowing and, although smaller, they can compare favourably in colour and perfume with any hot-house-grown blooms. They are generally offered as Giant Chabaud or Marguerite Carnations, and can be obtained in separate colours or mixed. These are magnificent for

9. Dianthus Heddewigii *var.* laciniatus. *A particularly showy strain, bearing large flowers with fringed petals. Fine for bedding and massing.*

50

bedding or cutting, especially if disbudded. Sow in gentle heat in February, grow on in small pots and plant out in April, 1½–2 ft. *D. chinensis* var. *Heddewigii,* better known as 'Japanese Pinks'. Many varieties of lovely double and single flowers in a wide range of colours, 9 in. Cultivation as above. These lovely pinks can justifiably be considered as some of our most attractive annuals. *Dianthus* Sweet Wivelsfield, a lovely hybrid pink which resembles a Sweet William and can well be treated as an annual, 1½ ft. **Didiscus,** *see* Trachymene.

Dimorphotheca (Cape Marigold) (HHA) (Some species have been transferred to Osteospermum but are here re-

10. Dimorpho- theca *hybrids are among the most brilliantly coloured of all South African annuals, and a selection of these should be grown in every garden.*

ferred to as Dimorphotheca.) Among the brilliant annuals from S. Africa, the Dimorphothecas are outstanding for their vividly coloured flowers and are easily cultivated. They are sun lovers, and will not be a success during a dull, wet summer. Sow under glass in March and plant out in May. Magnificent for massing or bedding. *D. aurantiaca* (syn. *Castalis Tragus*), single, daisy-like flowers, rich golden-orange, bloom throughout the summer, 1–1½ ft.; *D. aurantiaca* hybrids, a mixture of yellow, orange, pink and white shades; *D. Barberiae* (syn. *Osteospermum Barberiae*), deep pinkish-purple, 1–2 ft.; *D. chrysanthemifolia,* foliage resembles that of a chrysanthemum, large yellow flowers on long stalks, a good pot plant, 2ft.; *D. Ecklonis* (syn. *Osteospermum Ecklonis*), a large, shrubby plant, white flowers with a blue eye, 2 ft.; *D. pluvialis* (syn. *D. annua*), large, single white blooms with reverse of petals shaded violet, 1–2 ft.

Dracocephalum (Dragonhead) (HA *or* P) Spikes of violet-blue flowers. Free blooming, dwarf, bushy habit. Sow outdoors in April. *D. Moldavica,* lovely shade of blue, suitable for half shade, July and August, 1–1½ ft.

Dragonhead, *see* Dracocephalum.

Eccremocarpus (P) Useful and easily grown climber with orange and scarlet tubular flowers, 1 in. long, in racemes. Requires a sheltered, sunny position. Sow in heat in March and plant out fairly large pot-grown plants in June. *E. scaber* (Chilean Glory Flower), the best species to grow as an annual, up to 15 ft.; the variety *aurea* is a lovely shade of yellow. If winter protection can be provided, plants will live for many years.

Echium (Viper's Bugloss) (B, HHA *or* P) Mostly perennials or even shrubs. *E. plantagineum,* worth growing as an annual for its handsome blue flowers. Sow under glass in March. Bushy, free-flowering plant, spikes of purple-blue flowers, excellent for bedding and pots, 1½ ft.

Egg Plant, *see* Solanum.

Emilia (Tassel Flower) (HHA) Small but vividly coloured flowers. The plants are so easy to grow that there is a certain risk of them becoming a nuisance, as they seed so freely and germinate anywhere. Self-sown seedlings, produced from plants which have flowered and seeded in July, will bloom in October. Strangely enough, these attractive plants are rarely seen in private gardens, although they are fine subjects for bedding. Sow out of doors in April. *E. sagittata* (syn. *E. flammea*), scarlet, tassel-like flowers at the end of long stems, 1½ ft. The variety *aurea* has bright, golden-orange-coloured blooms.

Eschscholzia (Californian Poppy) (HA) These are so widely grown that they hardly need any introduction, although the full range of types and colours may not be generally appreciated. All are sun lovers and are tolerant of even the poorest soil. Sow at intervals in the open ground during March and April for flowers throughout the summer. They are not suitable for transplanting. For detailed descriptions of named varieties see seedsmen's lists. *E. caespitosa,* a gem among the dwarf species, small yellow flowers, ideal for the rock garden, 4–6 in.; *E. californica,* most present-day garden hybrids have come from this large, yellow-flowered species, now obtainable in orange, flame, copper, pink, cream, red, yellow and white shades in the following forms: tall, 1 ft.; dwarf, 9 in.; double flowered, 9 in.; *E. tenuifolia*, a small, compact, miniature species with tiny, bright yellow flowers, a first-class plant for the rock garden or for edging, 3–5 in.; sow in open ground in April.

Euphorbia (Spurge) (HHA) Chiefly grown for its ornamental green and scarlet leaves. Sow in open ground in April. *E. heterophylla* (Mexican Fire-plant). Flowers inconspicuous, orange-red, 2 ft.

Evening Primrose, *see* Oenothera biennis.

Everlasting Flowers, *see* Chapter Four.

Exacum (HHA *and* P) Only suited for the greenhouse. Blue, star-like flowers, sweetly scented. Sow in April and grow in pots for summer flowering. *E. affine*, bluish-lilac, June–October, 6–9 in.

False Daisy, *see* Bellium.

Felicia (HHA *and* B) Lovely little plants with blue, daisy-like flowers in summer. Useful for edging, the rock garden and window-boxes. Sow under glass in March. Require good soil and a warm sunny position. *F. Bergeriana*, dwarf, very free-flowering, bright blue, 4–6 in., excellent for rock garden and carpeting; *F. rotundifolia* (syn. *Aster rotundifolia*), ideal for bedding or edging, also a good subject for groundwork, clear blue, 9–12 in.

Flax, *see* Linum.

Flos Flower, *see* Ageratum.

Fountain Plant, *see* Amaranthus salicifolius.

Four o'clock Plant, *see* Mirabilis.

French Marigold, *see* Tagetes patula.

Gaillardia (HHA *or* P) Among the most brilliantly coloured of all border plants. Flowers produced throughout the summer and autumn. Excellent for cut blooms. Sow under glass in March and plant out about May. *G. amblyodon,* smallish, blood-red flowers, 2–3 ft.; *G. pulchella,* large flowered, crimson with tips of petals yellow, 2 ft. There are many varieties in red, golden, yellow, reddish-brown scarlet and creamy-white.

Gaura (HA *or* P) Handsome plants with tall, slender stems bearing quantities of small, white and pink flowers. Effective in mixed borders or large beds. Flowers throughout the summer and autumn. Sow in open ground in April. *G. Lindheimeri,* the most decorative species, white and rose, July–October, 3–5 ft.

Gazania (Treasure Flower) (P) Almost prostrate plants with large, brilliantly coloured flowers like very big daisies. Needs full sun in hot, dry position. Mostly perennials requiring winter protection. To cultivate as annuals sow under glass in February or March, grow on in small pots and plant out in May. *G. splendens,* hybrids of this species are available in lovely shades of yellow, orange and red, and the flowers are often spotted with green or black. First-class for edging or bedding, summer, 6–9 in.

Gilia (HA, B *or* P) Small but freely produced flowers which require to be massed to obtain the best results. Well suited for edging. *G. achilleaefolia,* bushy habit, violet-blue flowers, August, 1 ft.; a white form, var. *alba.*; *G. androsacea,* erect growth, lilac to pinkish white in colour, August, 1–1½ ft.; *G. dianthoides* (syn. *Fenzlia dianthiflora*), useful as a greenhouse plant, lilac and yellow, July, 6 in.; *G. liniflora,* bushy habit, white, 1 ft.; *G. tricolor,* white and purple with yellow eye, 1 ft.

Glaucium (Horned Poppy) (HA *or* B) Handsome, large-flowered, poppy-like plants with long, horn-shaped seed-pods. Can be found growing wild in some districts of the British Isles, especially near the sea. Good garden plants of easy culture. Sow in open ground in March. Does not transplant well. *G. corniculatum,* orange-red with black marks at base of petals, 1 ft.; *G. flavum* (syn. *G. luteum*), yellow, ideal for dry, sandy soil, 2 ft.

Godetia (HA) Of great value for summer bedding and as pot plants for the greenhouse. Easy to grow and available in many colours. For indoor culture sow in October in gentle heat. For out of doors sow in open ground in March in warm, sunny position. *G. amoena,* crimson flowers, mid-summer 1–2 ft.; *G. grandiflora* (syn. *Oenothera Whitneyi*), large, rosy-red flowers with deeper centres, 1–2 ft. This species has been used to raise many garden hybrids, the taller of which vary from 2–3 ft., while there are dwarfer forms from 8–12 in. Colours range from crimson through pink to white.

Gomphrena Globosa (HHA) Several varieties of 'Everlasting Flowers'. Excellent for drying, ball-shaped blooms, white, yellow, pink or purple, 1½–2 ft. Sow under glass in March and plant out in May. *G. globosa* var. *rubra* is a dwarf form for edging, purple, 6 in.

Groundsel, *see* Senecio.

Gypsophila (HA *or* P) Chiefly grown for the light and graceful flowers which are so useful for mixing with other flowers. Most effective in the mixed border. Sow in open ground in April. *G. elegans,* delicate, cloud-like white flowers, June–October, 1½ ft.; var. *grandiflora* has larger flowers; var. *carminea,* pale pink; *G. muralis,* dwarf species suitable for the rock garden, pale pink, 6 in.; *G. viscosa* (syn. *G. rosea*), pink, scented flowers throughout the summer, 1–1½ ft.

Heartsease, *see* Viola.

Hebenstretia (HHA *or* P) An uncommon plant with slender spikes of veronica-like flowers. Suitable for pot culture or bedding. Sow out of doors in April or May. *H. comosa,* spikes of white flowers, spotted orange, fragrant, mid-summer, 1½–2 ft.

Helenium (Sneezeweed) (HA *or* P) Mostly hardy perennials, but there is one attractive annual species. Sow outside in March or April. *H. tenuifolium,* bushy habit, large, golden-yellow flowers in mid-summer, 1–1½ ft.

Helianthus (Sunflower) (HA *or* P) Among the annual sunflowers probably the best known is the old-fashioned giant *H. annuus* (Common Sunflower), the seeds of which are edible and enjoyed by parrots. There are also several other worth-while species, but they require plenty of room and are not particularly suitable for a very small garden. Sow in open ground in April. *H. annuus,* a real giant up to 10 ft. Huge yellow flowers often 1 ft. in diameter; *H. argophyllus,* yellow flowers and pleasing silvery coloured foliage, 8 ft.; *H. debilis,* a more compact species which requires less room, large quantities of small yellow flowers; also several nurserymen's varieties in shades of red, orange, bronze and cream, 3–4 ft.

Helichrysum (Everlasting Flower) (HHA *or* P) These provide some of the best of the so-called 'Everlasting Flowers' which are so popular for drying. Sow in open ground in April, or to obtain earlier results sow under glass in March and plant out in May. Best effects will be obtained from a rich soil, and a sunny position is essential. Excellent for the mixed border. *H. bracteatum,* the best species for growing as an annual, single, golden-yellow flowers, and white, scarlet and red varieties, 2–3 ft. The variety *monstrosum* has large, double blooms; the best for cutting. Yellow, orange, white, pink and crimson forms.

Heliophila (HHA)   Excellent as greenhouse pot plants or for borders and bedding. Sow several seeds in small pots in March and either grow on for planting out in May or pot on for indoor work. *H. leptophyla,* blue with a white eye, bushy habit, 9 in.; *H. linearifolia,* vivid blue flowers, 1 ft. Both require full sun.

Helipterum Australian Everlasting Flower) (HA)   This name now includes **Acroclinium** and **Rhodanthe** and forms a lovely genus of 'Everlasting Flowers'. First-class garden plants, of graceful and pleasing appearance. Easy to grow in dry, sunny positions. Sow under glass in March and plant out in May. Summer flowering. *H. Humboldtianum,* clusters of small yellow flowers, 9 in.; *H. Manglesii* (*Rhodanthe Manglesii*), white, pink or red flowers, the best of the genus for cutting, 1–1½ ft.; *H. roseum* (*Acroclinium roseum*), very showy, large, single pink flowers. There is also a double form of greater value as the blooms are less likely to close in dull weather. White and pink variations are obtainable, 1–1½ ft.

Hemp, *see* Cannabis sativa.

Hibiscus (P *or* HHA) Some of the most beautifully coloured of all popular garden plants, a few of which may be grown as annuals. Sow in heat in February, grow on in pots and plant out in May. *H. esculentus* is often

11. Hibiscus trionum. *A very lovely, half-hardy annual. Sulphur - yellow flowers with a contrasting purple eye.*

grown in the vegetable garden, for the long, green edible seed-pods known as 'Okra' or 'Gumbo', handsome flowers of a beautiful clear yellow, 5 ft.; *H. Manihot*, lovely lemon-yellow blooms 5 in. in diameter with deep crimson centre, late summer, 3–4 ft.; *H. Trionum* (syn. *H. africanus*), smaller flowers; yellow with purple eye, 1½ ft.
Honesty, *see* Lunaria biennis.

Hop, *see* Humulus.

Horned Poppy, *see* Glaucium.

Humulus (Hop) (P) Well worth growing, a most ornamental, fast-growing vine. Ideal for quickly covering fences, etc. Sow under glass in April and plant out at end of May. The seed vessels are most attractive in autumn. *H. lupulus,* attractive, light green leaves. The variety *aureus* has golden-coloured foliage.

Hunnemannia (P) A very tender but beautiful plant with glaucous green, feathery leaves and lovely, yellow, poppy-like flowers in late summer. Also useful as a pot plant. Requires full sun in a well-drained position on sandy soil. Sow under glass in March and plant out in May. *H. fumariifolia,* compact, bushy habit, 1½ ft.

Iberis (Candytuft) (B, P *or* HA) Ideal for bedding, edging or window-boxes. Long flowering period and easy to grow. Sow in open ground in March. *I. amara,* large heads of white flowers, 1–1½ ft.; var. 'Little Prince', 6 in.; *I. umbellata* (Common Candytuft), purple, 1 ft. Numerous garden forms are obtainable ranging in height from 6–12 in., colours include pink, lilac, carmine and white.

Ice Plant, *see* Mesembryanthemum crystallinum.

Iceland Poppy, *see* Papaver nudicaule.

Impatiens (Balsam) (HHA) Beautiful old-fashioned favourites which appear to be losing some of their popularity. Sow in heat in early April and grow on in pots, plant out in late May in a warm, protected situation. They are more difficult to grow than many other annuals, but are free flowering over a long period. Excellent as pot-grown plants under glass. *I. Balsamina,* this species has provided the hybrid strain *Camelliaeflora,* and includes pink, scarlet and white, double, free-flowering forms, 1½ ft.; *I. Delavayi,* flowers yellow marked with purple, late flowering, 3–4 ft.; *I. Holstii,* large scarlet flowers, 2–3 ft.; *I. Roylei,* robust species suitable for partial shade, purple and white, 3–4 ft.

Indian Corn, *see* Zea.

Ionopsidium (HA) Easily grown, dainty little plants, ideal for the rock garden, edging or in paving. Sow in flowering positions in March or April. Prefer a moist, shady

12. Ipomoea tricolor (*Convolvulus*). *One of the most showy of all annual climbers. Clear, sky-blue flowers veined with pink. Vigorous growth and free flowering.*

position. *I. acaule* (Carpet Plant), dwarf carpeter, violet-blue, useful for pots and boxes, 3 in.

Ipomoea (Bindweed, Morning Glory, Convolvulus) (HHA *or* P) Lovely twining climbers with large, vividly coloured flowers. Ideal for pergolas and trellis-work. All very fast growing, enjoying full sun in a warm position. Sow under glass in March, 4 or 5 seeds in a small pot, and plant out in late May or June. *I. hederacea*, large blue or purple flowers; also various nurserymen's varieties; *I. purpurea* (Morning Glory), grown under the name *Convolvulus major*, white, violet, pink, purple, crimson, red and dark blue; one of the finest of all annual climbers; *I. tricolor*, until recently known as *I. rubro-caerulea*, huge flowers of incredibly, clear sky-blue. Thrives best during a hot, dry summer. 'Heavenly Blue' is noteworthy.

Jacobaea, *see* Senecio.

Jewel of the Veldt, *see* Ursinia.

Kochia (Summer Cypress) (HA) Of little value as a flowering plant, but probably the finest of all annuals grown for their foliage. Forms compact, pale green bushes, the feathery foliage turns a glorious, crimson-red in autumn. Suitable for growing as specimen plants or massing in bedding, will sometimes reach a height of 3 ft. with a diameter of 2 ft., seeds itself easily. *K. Scoparia tricophylla*, the most suitable species for general purposes, sow under glass in March or in open ground in April.

Larkspur, *see* Delphinium.

Lathyrus odoratus (Sweet Pea), *see* Chapter Two.

Lavatera (Mallow) (P *or* HA) One species is a true

annual, and its varieties are among the most beautiful plants suitable for growing as annuals. Sow where the plants are to flower, either in April or in protected places in September. The latter will flower earlier and produce more vigorous plants. Rich soil is appreciated, in a warm, sunny position. Easy to cultivate but requires plenty of room and careful staking. *L. trimestris* (*L. rosea*), rose flowers produced in great profusion, June–October, 3–6 ft.; vars. *alba*, large white flowers; 'Loveliness', an excellent variety, with large, richer coloured rose-pink blooms and a more compact habit. Ideal for massing.

Layia (HA) Easily grown, dwarf, early flowering plants, but only of modest value. Sow in open ground from March to June. *L. calliglossa*, small plant, 1 ft. high covered with little yellow, daisy-like flowers; *L. elegans*, the most attractive species, greyish foliage, yellow and white blooms, 1 ft.; *L. glandulosa*, white, 6–18 in.

Leptosyne (HHA) Rather difficult, but worth trying for their large and very handsome, daisy-shaped flowers and decorative foliage. Require good soil in warm position in full sun. Sow under glass in March and grow on as pot plants until planted out in late May. Flowers from midsummer onwards. *L. calliopsidea*, large, rich yellow blooms, 1–1½ ft.; *L. maritima*, requires less sun than the other species, golden-yellow, 2–3 ft.; *L. Stillmanii*, the best species, intense yellow flowers, 1–2 ft.

Limnanthes (HA) Dwarf, easily grown and early flowering. Useful for massing, rock gardens and edging. Any soil and sunny position. For earliest flowers sow in permanent position in open ground in September, otherwise out of doors in April. *L. Douglasii,* scented, yellow and white flowers, 6 in.

Linaria (Toadflax) (HA *or* P) Effective and easily grown plants, mostly dwarf or prostrate. Excellent for massing at edge of borders and for rock gardens. Sow in open ground in March or April. Flower throughout the early summer. *L. alpina,* one of the most beautiful of all alpines with its trailing habit and masses of tiny, violet and orange flowers, the variety *rosea* is bright pink and orange; *L. maroccana,* magnificent annual species, purple-red, 1 ft. Many attractive varieties, such as *alba,* white; 'Ruby King', blood-red; and mixtures including orange, yellow, pink, purple and red; *L. reticulata,* purple and yellow, 2–2½ ft.

Linum (Flax) (HA) Very easy to grow and free flowering. Sow in open ground in April. *L. grandiflorum,* comparatively large, red flowers, also white, pink and crimson forms, fine for massing, 1–2 ft.; *L. usitatissimum,* interesting for its economic value as flax is obtained from the plant fibres and linseed oil from the seed, flowers a delicate pale blue, 2 ft.

Lobelia (HHA *or* P) In some respects too easy to grow and their popularity has made some of the dwarf varieties monotonous. The taller ones are less common and several are of great beauty. Sow in gentle heat in February or March, and grow on either in pots or boxes until planted out in late May. Can also be used as pot plants in the greenhouse, while the dwarf ones are suitable for window-boxes and baskets. *L. cardinalis,* magnificent spikes of scarlet flowers, mid-summer, 1½–2½ ft.;

L. Erinus, parent of the popular blue, edging lobelia, 3–6 in. There are also numerous trade varieties in different shades of blue, some of which have a trailing habit; *L. siphilitica,* similar to *L. cardinalis* but with lovely blue flowers; the variety *alba* is white; *L. vedrariensis,* very fine, recently introduced French hybrid, similar to *L. cardinalis* but with rich purple flowers. The trio *L. cardinalis, L. syphilitica* and its variety *alba* are excellent for bedding together when a combination of red, white and blue is required. If protected during frosty weather, the plants can be grown as perennials.

Love-in-a-mist, *see* Nigella.

Love-lies-bleeding, *see* Amaranthus caudatus.

Luffa cylindrica (Luffa) (HHA) A fascinating, easily grown climber. Attractive yellow flowers and 1–1½ ft. long cucumber-like fruits which when ripe and dried in late summer provide the ordinary bath loofah. Requires rich soil in hot, sunny position on pergola, trellis or poles. Sow in greenhouse in March, 3 or 4 seeds per small pot and plant out in April or May.

Lunaria (Honesty) (HA) Attractive for its flowers and disk-like, transparent seed vessels about the size of a penny, which when dried are useful for indoor decoration. Sow in open ground in March. *L. annua* (syn. *L. biennis*), lilac or purple, June, 2–2½ ft.

Lupinus (Lupins) (HA *or* P) So much attention has been paid to perennial Lupins during recent years that the annual species have been neglected. They are, however, well worth cultivating, easy to grow and most attractive. Sow in open ground in April and thin out drastically.

L. densiflorus (syn. *L. Menziesii*), fragrant, yellow flowers in August, 1½–2 ft. ; *L. Hartwegii,* blue and white, 2–3 ft., and many vividly coloured varieties ideal for massing in beds or borders, late summer; *L. mutabilis* var. *Cruck-shanksii,* scented, violet and pink flowers, 4 ft.; *L. nanus,* a dwarf species, mauve and blue, 6–12 in.; and var. *albus,* white; *L. subcarnosus,* dark blue and white, dwarf, almost trailing habit.

Lychnis (Campion) (Including **Viscaria** (HA *or* P) Some of the most vividly coloured of all annuals and very easy to grow. Sow in open ground in March or April. Also suitable as greenhouse pot plants. *L. Coeli-rosa,* very long flowering period, carmine-red, 1 ft.; var. *alba,* white; *L. Coeli-rosa* var. *oculata* (better known as *Viscaria oculata*) has a vast range of vivid colours such as blue, purple, white, crimson and pink, and is ideal for massing.

Madwort, *see* Alyssum.

Maize, *see* Zea Mays.

Malcolmia (Virginia Stock) (HA) Almost too popular to need any recommendation. An infallible standby for edges and borders. Sow in autumn to have very early flowers, or in open ground in March for summer display. *M. maritima,* the species which has provided the present-day forms, obtainable in white, crimson, pink and pale yellow, 3–4 in.

Malope (HA) Introduced over 200 years ago, this fine annual is deservedly as popular as ever. Easy to grow in almost any soil, but prefers sun to shade. Long flowering period throughout the summer. Sow out of doors in April. *M. trifida,* big, pinkish-mauve flowers, fine for massing, 2–3 ft.; var. *grandiflora,* a richer colour; and *alba,* a white form.

Marguerite, *see* Chrysanthemum frutescens.

Marigold, *see* Tagetes and Calendula.

Marvel of Peru, *see* Mirabilis.

Mask Flower, *see* Alonsoa.

Matthiola (Stock) (HA, B *or* P) Popular and easily grown plants. Divided into two broad groups. Night-scented Stocks (*M. bicornis*) and Brompton Stocks (*M. incana*), of which the variety *annua* forms the strain known as 'Ten-week' or 'Intermediate' Stock. A combination of the various types will provide a brilliant display of bloom throughout the summer. They have a delicious perfume, are useful for cutting and some make good pot plants for the greenhouse. *M. bicornis* (Night-scented Stock), single flowers, dwarf, lilac-coloured flowers which open from sunset to dawn, sweetly scented, 1 ft. Sow in open ground March or April. *M. incana* (Brompton Stock), biennials or perennials. Sow in frames in July; grow on and transplant seedlings for plants to flower the following year. *M. incana* var. *annua* (Ten-week or Intermediate). Ten week Stocks are true annuals, large and mostly double flowers in a great range of colours, 1½–2 ft. Sow in cold frame in April and plant out in late May; Intermediate Stocks require a longer time to reach maturity and flowering stage, 1–1½ ft. Many colours. Sow in cold frame in July; transplant young seedlings to nursery beds in sheltered position for the winter. Plant out into flowering position in good soil in March for July and August flowering. If sown in open ground in March will bloom the following autumn. The most suitable Stocks for growing in pots for indoor use are the intermediate varieties. Sow in gentle heat in July for winter and early spring flowering. Transplant seedlings into small pots (3 to a pot) and continue to grow on and re-pot, without allowing them to become pot-bound, until 5- or 6-in.-size pots have been reached. During late summer and early autumn the pots can be kept outside or in a cool greenhouse to secure sturdy, robust plants.

Maurandya (HHA *or* P) Neglected but very lovely, free flowering climbers. Sow under glass in March and pot on young seedlings. Plant out in warm, sunny position in May or June. *M. Barclaiana,* violet-coloured flowers like a small Foxglove, climbs rapidly, summer flowering. Also a white form; *M. scandens* (syn. *M. erubescens*), larger and more vigorous, pink.

Mentzelia (Bartonia) (HA) Outstandingly beautiful plants with vividly coloured flowers. Excellent for bedding and greenhouse culture. *M. bartonioides,* the best species for pot culture, abundant, large yellow flowers, $1\frac{1}{2}$ ft. Sow in heat in February and pot on young plants as necessary. Can either be planted out in May or grown on to flower in pots. *M. Lindleyi* (*Bartonia aurea*), big, golden-yellow flowers, ideal for bedding or borders in warm, sunny position, sow in open ground in April, 1 ft.

Mesembryanthemum (HHA *or* P) Most of these magnificent plants are tender perennials; ideal for borders, bedding and the rock garden in localities which are rather mild during the winter. Some can also be effectively grown as pot plants, and a few can be treated as

13. Mentzelia bartonioides (Bartonia aurea). *A dwarf, first-rate plant for borders or bedding. Masses of large, golden-yellow flowers in mid-summer.*

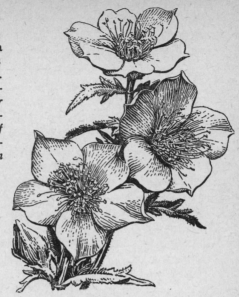

annuals. They have an abundance of brilliant flowers but require constant sun in a hot, dry position. Sow in heat in March and plant out in June. *M. criniflorum,* spreading habit, fine for rock garden, fleshy leaves and masses of mauve, pink, yellow or orange, star-like flowers, 4 in.; *M. crystallinum,* often known as 'Ice Plant' because the foliage has a shiny, ice-like appearance, small white flowers, 6 in.

Mexican Fire-plant, *see* Euphorbia heterophylla.

Mexican Poppy, *see* Argemone.

Mexican Sunflower, *see* Tithonia.

Mignonette, *see* Reseda.

Milkwort, *see* Polygala.

Mimulus (Monkey Flower, Musk) (HHA *or* P)   Interesting plants with curious flowers. Suitable for damp, semi-shady positions in borders and rock gardens. Ideal for growing in pots. Sow under glass in March and plant out in May. *M. brevipes* (Yellow Monkey Flower), large yellow blooms, 1 ft.; *M. cardinalis,* orange and scarlet, 1–2 ft.; *M. Fremontii,* large pink flowers, prefers drier and more sunny position, 9 in.; *M. luteus* (Monkey Flower), yellow blooms with crimson markings, 1–2 ft.; also many trade varieties. *M. moschatus,* the common Musk with the legendary perfume, a trailing plant, small yellow flowers, 6–9 in.; *M. Palmeri,* big yellow and red flowers, 1 ft.

Mina lobata, *see* Quamoclit lobata.

Mirabilis Jalapa (Four o'clock plant, Marvel of Peru) (P) A curious and beautiful plant which deserves to be more widely grown. Easily cultivated as an annual if grown in a warm, sunny position. Plants form small tubers, which can be lifted in autumn and stored in sand until the following spring. Sow under glass in March, grow on in small pots and plant out in May. Fragrant, funnel-shaped flowers, white, pink, red, yellow or striped, 2–3 ft. A curious feature about the very attractive blooms is that they do not open until the late afternoon, and then close again in the morning. This peculiarity can be exploited if the plants are grown in association with Portulaca, the flowers of which close in the late afternoon and open as soon as touched by the morning sun. The two plants will thus between them provide open blooms twenty-four hours a day, in day and night shifts.

Monkey Flower, *see* Mimulus.

Morning Glory, *see* Ipomoea.

Musk, *see* Mimulus moschatus.

Namaqualand Daisy, *see* Dimorphotheca aurantiaca.

Nasturtium, *see* Tropaeolum.

Nemesia (HHA) One of the first of the more modern S. African annuals to become popular in Great Britain, for borders and bedding, or for pots. Free flowering, brilliant colours and easy to grow. Sow under glass in April and plant out in May. Requires a warm, sunny position. *N. strumosa,* parent of most present-day hybrids. Original species mauve, yellow or white, but the modern, large-flowered hybrids can be obtained in almost every colour. Dwarf types, 6–9 in.; taller varieties, 1 ft.

Nemophila (Baby Blue Eyes) (HHA) Almost prostrate, spreading plants with pretty foliage and comparatively large, handsome flowers. Suitable for edges, boxes, pots or baskets and any odd space where there is plenty of sun but adequate moisture. Sow in flowering position in March or April. Established plants will often seed themselves. *N. maculata,* one of the prettiest of all dwarf annuals, white flowers with purple marks at tips of petals, summer, 6 in.; *N. Menziesii* (syn. *N. insignis*), unusually beautiful, bright blue flowers produced in abundance, spreading. There is also a white form.

Nicandra (Apple of Peru) (HA) Vigorous plants requiring plenty of room; well suited for borders. The Physalis-like seed vessels can be dried for indoor use. *N. Phys-*

alodes, attractive blue flowers, sow in open ground in March–April, summer, 3–4 ft.

Nicotiana (Tobacco) (HHA) An easily grown annual, the commercial tobacco plant (*N. tabacum*) is fairly widely cultivated. As a decorative plant it has little value, except for the enormous rather exotic leaves. Sow in gentle heat in April, and plant out in warm, sunny position in June. Gather leaves for drying in September. Many of the other species and varieties are of great beauty and can be included among the finest of all annuals. Culture as for *N. tabacum* or can be sown in open ground in late April. Will often seed themselves and come up year after year. *N. alata* var. *grandiflora* (*N. affinis*), large white flowers, strongly scented, 3–5 ft., var. 'Crimson Bedder', 1½ ft.; *N. Sanderae* hybrids, the best of all, very free flowering; crimson, pink or white, scented, 2–3 ft.

Nigella (Love-in-a-mist, Fennel-flower) (HA) A beautiful and easily grown annual. Excellent for bedding and cut blooms. Attractive, fennel-like foliage; blue flowers surrounded by green, feathery involucre. The large, bladder-like seed-pods are unusual. Sow in open ground in March. *N. damascena,* light blue, July, 1–2 ft.; *N. hispanica,* large pale blue flowers, summer, big seed-pods which can be dried for winter decoration indoors, 1–2 ft.; *N. sativa,* pale bluish-white, aromatic seeds, 1½ ft.

Night-scented Stock, *see* Matthiola bicornis.

Nolana (Chilean Bell-flower) (HA) A lovely plant with blue petunia-shaped flowers. Dwarf or trailing. Useful for edging, rock garden, pots or boxes. Sow outdoors in March; sunny position. *N. atriplicifolia* (*N. grandiflora*), bright blue flowers with pale yellow eye, mid-summer, 4–6 in.; *N. lanceolata,* the best species, with large, sky-blue flowers, mid-summer, 6 in.

Nycterinia, *see* Zaluzianskya.

Oenothera (Evening Primrose) (B, HA *or* P)   Valuable for the evening perfume of their large yellow flowers. Suitable for the mixed border, while several dwarf species can be used for the rock garden. Sow under glass in March and plant out in May. *O. acaulis* (*O. taraxacifolia*), prostrate, trailing habit, finely cut leaves, pinkish white flowers in summer, 6 in.; *O. biennis,* the best-known species; free-flowering and strong scent, yellow blooms, July–October, 5–6 ft.; the variety *Lamarckiana* has larger flowers and is of a dwarfer habit; *O. bistorta,* rich yellow, summer, 1–2 ft.; *O. Drummondii,* pale yellow flowers up to 3 in. in diameter, July and August, 1 ft.; *O. missouriensis,* ideal for the rock garden, big yellow flowers throughout the summer, 4–6 in.; *O. tetraptera,* white, 1 ft., var. *rosea,* pink; *O. trichocalyx,* strongly scented white flowers in summer, 1–2 ft.

Okra, *see* Hibiscus esculentus.

Opium Poppy, *see* Papaver somniferum.

Osteospermum, *see* Dimorphotheca.

Oxalis (Wood Sorrel) (HA *or* P)   Pretty leaves and charming flowers but they can become troublesome weeds. Sow out of doors in March. Can also be grown from small bulbs. *O. rosea,* pink, spring flowering, useful for the rock garden and for growing in pots, 6 in.; *O. valdiviensis,* yellow, summer, 6 in.

Pansy, *see* Viola.

Papaver (Poppy) (HA *or* P)   If size of flowers, easiness of cultivation and colour ranges are standards by which annuals are judged, then the poppies which can be grown as annuals should be put at the top of the list. There are species and varieties from 6 in. to 6 ft. in height that can be brought into flower in summer from seed sown in the open ground in March or April. All prefer an open, sunny, well-drained position. *P. alpinum,* orange, yellow, salmon or white flowers, a gem for the rock garden, 6 in.; *P. glaucum, c*rimson, tulip-like flowers in mid-summer, 2 ft.; *P. nudicaule* (Iceland Poppy), yellow, orange, white or pink varieties, mid-summer, 1 ft. Many nurserymen's forms and varieties. Better results will be obtained if sown in frames in July and the young seedlings planted in their flowering positions in September; *P. pavoninum,* scarlet and black, 1–1½ ft.; *P. Rhoeas,* the wild 'Corn Poppy', scarlet, 1–2 ft. These will also give better results from an autumn sowing in open ground. Our present-day race of Shirley poppies have all been raised from this species and the story of how this was achieved by the late Rev. Wilks of Shirley over 50 years ago, is one of the greatest romances of plant hybridizing and selection, and the results are a fitting tribute to the memory of a patient and observant man. *P. somniferum* (Opium Poppy), the giant of the family, up to 6 ft. in height with lovely, pinkish-mauve flowers 4–5 in. in diameter, and coarse, glaucous green foliage, mid-summer. Most effective in beds or grouped in borders.

Penstemon (Beard Tongue) (P)   Particularly well suited for bedding. Sow in gentle heat in February, plant out young, pot-grown plants in May in full sun. *P. Hartwegii,* the only really suitable species for growing as an annual, 2½ ft. Available in a mixture of colours, mid-summer.

Petunia (P) The most good-natured, easily grown, weather-resisting, free-flowering and attractively coloured plant I know of for annual bedding. High praise indeed, but experience has shown that their value cannot be over-estimated. The single-flowered bedding varieties are particularly good, and even after a week's rain the plants and flowers will recover within a matter of hours. They are also excellent for baskets and window-boxes. Sow in slight heat in March and plant out in May in a sunny position. Will continue flowering from July until the beginning of winter. Most seedsmen offer a wide range of types, including large-flowered double; trailing or balcony; single bedding; dwarf compact; and the colours range from white to scarlet and pink to purple.

Phacelia (HA *or* P) For richness of colouring this lovely, gentian-blue flowered annual has few equals. Sow in open ground in April for summer flowering. *P. campanularia,* vivid blue, excellent for edges of carpeting, very free flowering, 8 in.; *P. congesta,* lavender-blue in June, 1 ft.; *P. Parryi,* violet-blue, 1 ft.; *P. tanacetifolia,* lilac-blue flowers in conspicuous clusters, 2–3 ft.; *P. Whitlavia,* large violet-blue flowers, 1 ft., var. *alba,* white.

Pheasant's Eye, *see* Adonis.

Phlox Drummondii (HHA) Sow under glass in March or April and plant out in May or June. Easy to grow and produce a mass of vividly coloured flowers throughout the summer. Prefer a warm, sunny position. The various trade catalogues offer two forms: large-flowered, 1–1½ ft., and dwarf, 6 in., both of which embrace such colours as white, yellow, pink, scarlet, violet, etc.

Pimpernel, *see* Anagallis.

Pink, *see* Dianthus.

Platystemon californicus (Cream Cups) (HA) Not often seen in gardens, but well worth growing for its small, poppy-like, pale yellow flowers which make a pleasing contrast with the greyish-green leaves. Sow out of doors in April, July–August, 6–9 in.

Polygala lutea (Milkwort) An annual species in a large genus of herbaceous perennials and shrubs. Abundance of orange flowers. Sow in open ground in April, 9 in.

Poor Man's Orchid, *see* Schizanthus.

Poppy, *see* Papaver.

Poppy Mallow, *see* Callirhoë.

Portulaca (Sun Plant) (HHA) For some reason this free-flowering and magnificently coloured annual is not grown in anything like the quantity its usefulness and beauty warrants. Perhaps it is the uncertain English climate which has made gardeners shy of Portulaca, for it certainly needs a hot, dry summer to produce the abundance of flowers which make it such a wonderful sight. The blooms are reluctant to open in dull weather and always close at dusk. (See further note in description of Mirabilis). Plants form a prostrate, spreading carpet of tiny, reddish-green leaves which, throughout the summer, are practically hidden by the masses of vividly coloured flowers, about the size of a penny, either single or double. The blooms are of the most intense hues and seem to

14 and 15. Portulaca
grandiflora.

*Dwarf plants with a
wide range of the
most vividly coloured
flowers. Single and
double f l o w e r e d
forms. Ideal for a
hot, dry, sunny posi-
tion.*

include every tint except blue. It is ideal for carpeting, edging, bedding or the rock garden. Sow in moderate heat in March and plant out in May in a warm, sunny position, preferably on light, well-drained soil. *P. grandiflora* has provided most of the present-day garden hybrids.

Prickly Poppy, *see* Argemone.

Quamoclit (HHA) Greenhouse, annual climbers which can, under favourable conditions, be grown out of doors. Of great beauty and useful for pergolas and pillars. Sow under glass in March and plant out young, pot-grown plants when all risk of cold weather is past. *Q. lobata* (*Mina lobata*), extremely beautiful with masses of small, scarlet and yellow flowers, but requires a sheltered position and warm, sunny weather.

Ragwort, *see* Senecio.

Reseda (Mignonette) (P) An old-fashioned favourite which, during the past 150 years, has remained one of the most popular plants grown for its scent. Ideal for bedding or pots. Sow in slight heat in March and grow on in pots, which if desired can be planted out in May. *R. odorata,* the parent of most varieties now in commerce, yellowish-white, 1–1½ ft.; vars. 'Crimson Giant', 1 ft.; 'Golden Queen', 9 in.; 'Machet Giant', light red, best for pot culture; and many other trade varieties.

Rhodanthe, *see* Helipterum.

Ricinus communis (Castor Oil Plant) (HHA) In English gardens grown only as a foliage plant. Its large, reddish-green leaves are most effective whether cultivated as a greenhouse pot plant or used as a bedding plant out of doors. In warmer countries it is grown for the seeds, which give a high yield of oil. Sow under glass in March and plant out in May, 2–5 ft. Among the varieties usually catalogued are: *Gibsonii,* with dark, almost purple foliage; *sanguineus,* reddish leaves; and *zanzibarensis,* a mixture of many colours.

Rocket Larkspur, *see* Delphinium Ajacis.

Rock Purslane, *see* Calandrina.

Rudbeckia (Coneflower) (HA *or* P)　Lovely, yellow, daisy-like flowers of particular value, as they flower so profusely in late summer and even into autumn. Excellent for bedding, borders and for naturalizing at the edge of rough grass or near groups of shrubs. The flowers are also excellent for cutting. Sow in open ground in March or April. *R. amplexicaulis,* yellow with maroon eye, 1–2 ft.; *R. bicolor,* yellow, very dark purple eye, 1–1½ ft., the var. 'Kelvedon Star' is particularly fine; *R. hirta* (Black-eyed Susan), yellow, dark brown centre, 1–1½ ft.

Sage, *see* Salvia.

Salpiglossis (HHA)　For richness and variety of colouring these have few equals. Large, trumpet-shaped flowers in crimson, blue, orange, scarlet, pink and yellow, each of which is veined with a contrasting shade. Magnificent as pot plants and for bedding, when their tall, erect flower stems are seen to perfection. Prefer rich, well-prepared soil in warm, sheltered position. Sow under glass in March and plant out pot-grown plants in June. *S. sinuata,* most modern varieties have come from this species, 2–2½ ft.

Saltbush, *see* Atriplex.

Salvia (HA, HHA *or* P)　Apart from the ever-popular *S. splendens,* several very attractive salvias can be grown as annuals. They are easy to cultivate, free-flowering and continue to provide a fine display until well into autumn. Well suited for individual beds or mixed borders. Sow in gentle heat in February and plant out pot-grown plants at end of May. *S. carduacea,* downy leaves, lavender-blue flowers, 1 ft. This species is best sown in open ground in April; *S. farinacea,* violet-blue, attractive leaves which appear to have been dusted with flour, 2½ ft.; *S. Horminum,* this species may also be sown in open ground in April, mauve-lavender, red or blue, 1–1½ ft. See trade catalogues for details of various forms; *S. splendens,* probably the only annually grown plant which has ever been a serious rival to the geranium as a red-flowered plant for formal bedding. In some respects it is more useful than the geranium, as it is more tolerant of shade.

Sand Verbena, *see* Abronia.

Sanvitalia procumbens (HA)   Dwarf, trailing habit, freely produced, daisy-like flowers, yellow with purple centre, 6 in. Sow out of doors in April. Suitable for the rock garden. Late summer. There is a double-flowered form.

Saponaria (Soapwort) (HA *or* P)   Very easy to grow, suitable for borders. Sow out of doors in April. *S. calabrica,* deep pink, mid-summer, 6–12 in. Also white and scarlet forms; *S. Vaccaria,* the most widely grown species because of its value for cutting, pink, 2½ ft.

Scabiosa (Sweet Scabious) (HA *or* P)   The wild scabious which is so attractive in our meadows is lovely enough, but the present-day hybrids are among the most beautiful of all popular garden plants. Their long stems make them excellent for cutting and ideal for beds or borders. In colour they range through blue, pink, crimson, purple, white and yellow. Height varies from 9 in. to 2 ft. *S. atropurpurea,* the parent of most garden forms, July–September, 2 ft. Sow under glass in March and plant out in May or sow in open ground in April.

Scarlet Flax, *see* Linum grandiflorum *var.* rubrum.

Schizanthus (Butterfly Flower; Poor Man's Orchid) (HHA) One of the finest of all annuals for growing as a pot plant in the cool greenhouse, but too susceptible to damage from bad weather to justfy recommendation as an out-of-doors bedding plant. For indoor purposes sow under glass in August. *S. Grahamii,* mauve and orange, 2 ft. Various hybrid varieties; *S. pinnatus,* violet, yellow, pink, 1–1½ ft.; *S. wisetonensis,* white, pink, crimson, 1 ft.

Schizopetalon Walkeri (HHA) Sweetly scented plumes of white flowers, mid-summer, 1 ft. Suitable for front of border. Sow under glass in March and plant out in May.

Sedum caeruleum (HA) A lovely little annual for the rock garden or for bedding. Pale blue flowers, late summer, 2–3 in. Sow in open ground in April.

Senecio (Cineraria, Groundsel, Ragwort) (HA, HHA *or* P) A huge genus of nearly 1,500 species, comparatively few of which are suitable or worth while as annual bedding plants. One of the best-known Senecios is *S. cruentus* and its hybrids, which have given us the modern cinerarias, among the most effective of all pot-grown annuals for the cold greenhouse during the winter months. They embrace a variety of types from 1–3 ft. in height and range through a vivid selection of blues, pink, crimsons and white. Seedsmen offer large-flowered and the smaller-bloomed stellata types. Sow under glass from April to August for a supply of flowering plants from September to March. Pot-grown plants raised from seed sown under glass in autumn can be used for bedding in early summer. *S. elegans* (*Jacobaea elegans*), daisy-like blooms in mid-summer, excellent for mixed border and cutting, 1–2 ft. Sow under glass in March and plant out in May. Deep pink with yellow eye.

Shirley Poppy, *see* Papaver Rhoeas.

Siberian Wallflower, *see* Cheiranthus Allionii.

Silene (Catchfly) (HA *or* P)   Old-fashioned favourites and still of great garden value, especially the dwarf ones for edging and rock gardens. Sow under glass in April and plant out in late May. Can also be sown in open ground in autumn. *S. Armeria*, clusters of rich purple flowers, 1–1½ ft.; *S. Asterias*, purple-pink, mid-summer, 2 ft.; *S. pendula*, double and single forms, white, salmon, pink and purple, 8–12 in.

Slipper Flower, *see* Calceolaria.

Snapdragon, *see* Antirrhinum.

Sneezeweed, *see* Helenium.

Soapwort, *see* Saponaria.

Solanum (HHA *or* P)   An enormous genus containing over a thousand species which include such well-known subjects as potatoes and the egg-plant. Many have attractive flowers and decorative berries, and are excellent for cultivation as greenhouse plants, while at least one is a fine annual bedder. *S. citrullifolium*, deeply lobed, spiny leaves, white or pale mauve flowers throughout the summer, 2–3 ft. In autumn masses of bright scarlet fruits like little tomatoes. Rather rampant but fine for massing where space is available. Sow under glass in March.

Specularia Speculum-Veneris (Venus's Looking Glass) (HA)   In spite of its alarming name, this is a humble little plant found wild in many parts of N. Europe, 9–12 in. Freely produced, violet-coloured, campanula-like flowers. Excellent for a cool, moist position in the rock garden or edge of border. Sow in open ground in March.

Spider Flower, *see* Cleome.

Spurge, *see* Euphorbia.

Stock, *see* Matthiola.

Stone Cress, *see* Aethionema.

Stonecrop, *see* Sedum.

Summer Cypress, *see* Kochia.

Sunflower, *see* Helianthus.

Sun Plant, *see* Portulaca.

Swan River Daisy, *see* Brachycome.

Sweet Alyssum, *see* Alyssum maritimum.

Sweet Pea, *see* Chapter Two.

Sweet Scabious, *see* Scabiosa.

Sweet Sultan, *see* Centaurea moschata.

Tagetes (Marigold) (HHA)   Easily grown plants particularly suited for massing in beds and for the mixed border. Sow under glass in March and plant out in May. Their vivid colouring calls for a certain amount of care to avoid clashes with other brightly coloured plants. Flowers last for most of the summer. *T. erecta* (African Marigold), pale yellow, 2–3 ft. Many seedsmen's varieties in different shades of orange, lemon and mixed. Also a dwarf form 1½ ft.; *T. lucida* (Mexican Marigold), a more pleasing scent than most, orange, 1–2 ft.; *T. patula* (French Marigold), dwarf, bushy plants, double and single, many varieties in yellow, orange and scarlet, and various combinations, 9–12 in.; *T. signata*, small flowers in great profusion, yellow, 1 ft., var. *pumila*, 9 in.

Tassel Flower, *see* Emilia.

Ten-week Stock, *see* Matthiola incana.

Thunbergia (Black-eyed Susan) (HHA *or* P) Fast-growing climbers well suited to trellis and pergolas, but require good weather and a warm, sunny position. Sow under glass in March and plant out young, pot-grown plants in June. *T. alata*, creamy-yellow flowers with an almost black throat; *T. Gibsonii*, vivid, orange flowers.

16. Thunbergia alata (*Black-eyed Susan*). *A handsome, free-flowering climber. Creamy-yellow flowers and a contrasting black centre.*

Tithonia (Mexican Sunflower) (HHA *or* P)   Probably the fastest growing and certainly one of the biggest annuals which can be cultivated in the average garden. Excellent for large borders or effective grown as individual, specimen plants, but must have plenty of room. Each plant can grow up to 9 ft. in height, with a diameter of 6–10 ft. It has a wide, branching habit and long, rigid flower stems terminating in large, orange, single zinnia-like blooms which are produced continuously from July to October. Sow under glass in March and plant out in May. *T. rotundifolia* (*T. speciosa*) the best species, flowers 3–4 in. in diameter.

Toadflax, *see* Linaria.

Tobacco Plant, *see* Nicotiana.

Trachelium caeruleum (P)   A fine, half-hardy herbaceous plant which can be grown as an annual. Suitable for bedding and also an excellent pot plant. Large heads of small blue flowers, 1–1½ ft. Also a white form. Sow in March and plant out pot-grown plants in May.

Trachymene (Blue Lace Flower) (HHA)   A most attractive plant with delicate, lace-like flowers. Very suitable for growing as a pot plant. When used for bedding out requires a hot, sunny position. Sow in greenhouse in March and plant out in May. *T. caerulea* (*Didiscus caerulea*), the choicest species, July, 10–15 in. *T. pilosa*, a dwarf species, mid-summer, 6 in.

Treasure Flower, *see* Gazania.

Tropaeolum (Nasturtium) (P)   Well-known and attractive plants with large, vividly coloured flowers and edible leaves. Climbing and bushy varieties, all very easy to grow. Suitable for pergolas, trellis, baskets, boxes and for bedding. Bloom throughout the summer. Tolerant of almost any type of soil. Sow in open ground in April. *T. majus* (Common Nasturtium), a vigorous climber, orange and yellow. From this species a wide range of modern garden forms has been evolved, the chief of which are as follows. For details of varieties of individual types see trade catalogues. Tall Climbing. Double Gleam, 12–18 in., semi-trailing. Tom Thumb or Dwarf, double or single flowered, 9 in. *T. peregrinum* (Canary Creeper), with small yellow flowers, is another vigorous climber which can reach a height of 10 ft.

Trumpet Flower, *see* Datura.

Ursinia (Jewel of the Veldt) (HHA)   Lovely South African plants which are now among our best annuals. Magnificent for bedding, edging, pot cultivation and, with the smaller species, the rock garden. Essentially sun lovers, they should be grown in light, well-drained soil. Apart from their delightful, daisy-like flowers, the finely cut foliage has considerable grace. Sow under glass in March and plant out in May, or sow in open ground in April. Bloom profusely throughout the summer. *U. anethoides*, one of the most handsome species, vivid orange flowers, red and black centres, good stems, 12–15 in.; *U. anthemoides*, yellow with purple centre, very free flowering, 1 ft.; *U. pulchra* (syn. *Sphenogyne speciosa*), a dwarf species, compact habit, orange flowers with black centre, 9 in.; *U. pygmaea*, orange-yellow, 6 in.

Valerian, *see* Centranthus.

Venidium (HHA *and* P)   A brightly coloured, daisy-like flower from S. Africa, with blooms far larger and more showy than ursinias or dimorphothecas. It is, however, a fine-weather plant and liable to be disappointing if used on a large scale during a bad summer. Require a light soil in a sheltered, sunny position. Sow under glass in April and plant out in late May. *V. decurrens* (*V. calendulaceum*), yellow with purple centre, 2 ft.; *V. fastuosum*, the most showy species with flowers up to 5 in. in diameter, rich orange with brown, black and purple centre, downy foliage, 2–2½ ft. Seedsmen now offer a strain which shows considerable colour variation; *V. macrocephalum*, pale yellow with dark brown eye, 2–2½ ft.

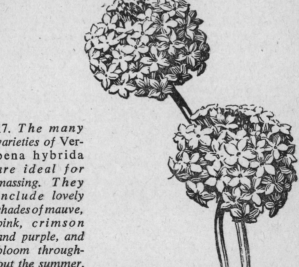

17. *The many varieties of* Verbena hybrida *are ideal for massing. They include lovely shades of mauve, pink, crimson and purple, and bloom throughout the summer.*

Venus's Looking Glass, *see* Specularia.

Verbascum (Mullein) (B *and* P) Lovely summer-flower-ing plants with blooms carried in tall, erect spikes. Mostly perennials but two can be cultivated as annuals. Prefer warm, sunny position in mixed borders or beds. Sow in open ground in April. *V. olympicum,* leaves form a large, compact rosette, yellow flower spikes, 5–6 ft.; *V. phoeniceum,* a dwarfer species, red, purple, pink, white and mauve, 2–3 ft.

Verbena (P) Dwarf, free flowering and vividly coloured plants valuable for massing in beds, edges of borders, window-boxes and baskets. Sow under glass in February and plant out in May. Full sun. Flowering period July-September. *V. hybrida* (syn. *V. hortensis*). Not a good botanical name, but the one generally used in the trade to describe the large-flowered garden varieties which have originated from crosses made between several species, notably *V. teucrioides.* Most of these are about 1 ft. in height and include every shade of pink, red, white and mauve. See catalogues for detailed descriptions of individual varieties. *V. venosa* (syn. *V. rigida*), a choice, smaller flowered species, rich violet-red, 10–12 in.

Vetch, *see* Vicia.

Vicia (Vetch) (HA *or* P) Somewhat rampant plants whose chief value lies in their ability to climb and rapidly cover trellis work, etc. Sow in open ground in April. *V. Cracca,* pinkish-mauve flowers rather like tiny sweet peas; *V. Gerardii,* blue flowers and small attractive foliage.

Viola (Pansy, Heartsease) (P) Of great value for carpet-ing, especially among spring-flowering bulbs, and for edging. For summer-flowering plants sow in open ground in April. For spring-flowering plants sow in cold frame in July and plant out in flowering positions in September or October. During a mild autumn and winter a considerable amount of bloom can be obtained by sowing in mid-summer a type of pansy known as winter flowering. None of these hybrid pansies have any authentic botanical name and their origin has become extremely confused. Nurserymen's seed lists contain a great many named varieties as well as mixtures in all shades.

Viper's Bugloss, *see* Echium.

Virginia Stock, *see* Malcolmia maritima.

Viscaria, *see* Lychnis.

Waitzia (HHA)   Uncommon 'Everlasting Flowers' of Australian origin and of attractive appearance. Sow under glass in April and plant out in late May in a dry, hot position. Excellent for cutting. *W. aurea,* golden-yellow, fine for massing, $1\frac{1}{2}$–2 ft.; *W. grandiflora,* large yellow flowers, 1–$1\frac{1}{2}$ ft.; *W. odontolepis,* white, 1–2 ft.; *W. Streetziana,* the smallest species, white, 6–9 in.

Wallflower, *see* Cheiranthus.

Woodruff, *see* Asperula.

Wood Sorrel, *see* Oxalis.

Xeranthemum (Immortelle) (HA)   An 'Everlasting Flower' of considerable garden merit. Ideal for the mixed border or for bedding as the flowering period is very long. Sow in open ground in April. *X. annuum,* large purple flowers, 2 ft. Numerous seedsmen's varieties in a considerable range of colours, with either single or double blooms.

Zaluzianskya (Nycterinia) (HHA)   Compact, miniature

little plants with tiny, sweetly scented flowers which open at night. Sow in greenhouse in March and plant out in May. Excellent for rock garden and edging. *Z. capensis* (syn. *Nycterinia capensis*), white and purple, early summer, 1 ft.; *Z. selaginoides* (syn. *Nycterinia selaginoides*), white and mauve, 6–9 in.

Zea Mays (Maize, Indian Corn) (HHA) This fast-growing giant of the grass family is sometimes grown to great advantage as an annual bedder or 'dot plant'. The long, broad, ribbon-like leaves are extremely attractive and are of a lovely shade of green. There is also a variegated form. In the British Isles plants do not flower as freely as in hotter countries and rarely exceed 3 or 4 ft. in height, but in warmer climates they will grow up to 10 ft. Sow in open ground in May.

Zinnia (HHA) Last in this alphabetical list but in my estimation one of the finest of all annuals. Both the giant and miniature flowered forms have a remarkable range of colouring, in tints which are rarely seen in any other blooms. The symmetrical formation of each flower is a thing of beauty in itself, while the long, rigid stems make them ideal for cutting. Zinnias like good living and adore the sun, so should only be grown in well-prepared soil in a warm, sunny situation. Broadcast the seed in cold frames towards the end of April, then plant out direct into flowering positions in late May or early June. Growth is generally so rapid that late planting is an advantage in order to avoid bad weather. They can also be sown in gentle heat in April; pricked out into boxes and planted in June. Zinnias are magnificent for bedding or the border, while the dwarf forms can be used for edging. During a hot, dry summer zinnias make a magnificent display, but to appreciate their maximum possibilities they should be seen flowering in warmer countries, where plants are often 4 or 5 ft. in height and blooms are

18. Zinnia Haageana. *A lovely little dwarf Zinnia with small, orange-scarlet flowers which remain in bloom throughout the summer. An ideal subject for bedding.*

frequently over 5 in. in diameter. Seed catalogues contain numerous garden forms, both double and single flowered. *Z. elegans*, the parent of most present-day garden hybrids, original species, 1–2 ft. Pinkish-purple flowers, single and rather small. Now available in the following forms:

Giant Double: Enormous double flowers but with

loose arrangement of petals. Sold as a mixture or in individual colours such as white, yellow, pink, orange, scarlet; 2-3 ft. Double: Similar to previous type but with petals more tightly arranged; 2 ft. Dahlia-flowered: Large flowered and with petals inclined to be raised; 2-3 ft. Double Dwarf Mixed: Dwarf, compact habit and big flowers; 1¼ ft. Sutton's Dwarf Hybrids: Small, double or single flowers; 9-12 in. Two very fine, miniature species zinnia are: *Z. Haageana,* a lovely little plant with compact habit and masses of small, orange-scarlet flowers, 9 in.; *Z. linearis,* a magnificent species for bedding. Compact habit, vivid orange flowers which individually last for weeks so that the plants are a mass of bloom from July to October. The flowers remain fresh for so long that it is quite difficult to collect seed; 6-9 in.